W9-AUD-823

Careers in Focus

ENTREPRENEURS

THIRD EDITION

Ferguson
An imprint of Infobase Publishing

Careers in Focus: Entrepreneurs, Third Edition

Ferguson
An imprint of Infobase Publishing
132 West 31st Street
New York NY 10001

Library of Congress Cataloging-in-Publication Data

Careers in focus. Entrepreneurs. — 3rd ed.
    p. cm.
  Includes index.
  ISBN-13: 978-0-8160-7303-0 (hardcover : alk. paper)
  ISBN-10: 0-8160-7303-1 (hardcover : alk. paper) 1. Vocational guidance—
Juvenile literature. 2. Entrepreneurship—Vocational guidance—Juvenile litera-
ture. I. Ferguson Publishing. II. Title: Entrepreneurs.
  HF5381.2.C376 2009
  331.702—dc22
                                        2009000798

Ferguson books are available at special discounts when purchased in bulk quantities for businesses, associations, institutions, or sales promotions. Please call our Special Sales Department in New York at (212) 967-8800 or (800) 322-8755.

You can find Ferguson on the World Wide Web at http://www.fergpubco.com

Text design by David Strelecky
Cover design by Alicia Post

Printed in the United States of America

MP MSRF 10 9 8 7 6 5 4 3 2 1

Table of Contents

Introduction

Entrepreneurs are people who set up and manage their own business enterprises—assuming the risks if they fail, reaping the rewards if they succeed. Owning a small business has been part of the American dream since the nation's earliest days, and the late 20th century saw a great increase in entrepreneurial ambition. This may be in part due to the downsizing trends of American companies. Whereas earlier in the century a person could work for one company until retirement, such job security has become more rare. It is increasingly common for men and women in their 50s to lose their jobs and find themselves with few job prospects. With severance pay in hand, these people often invest in the businesses they've longed for their whole lives, recognizing these ventures as no more risky than any other career pursuit. A generation ago, a person chose a job path and stuck with it; these days, people experiment with a variety of careers throughout their lives.

Today, more than 500 colleges and universities in the United States offer entrepreneurship courses—60 percent more than in 1984. There are also more organizations, periodicals, and Web pages advising people on how to start their businesses and keep them running. *Entrepreneur* and *Success* magazines publish special issues devoted to small business and maintain Web sites. The Small Business Administration (SBA) guarantees more than $12 billion in loans every year. The SBA also provides business start-up kits, workshops, and research assistance—including special programs for women and minorities.

Despite some discouraging statistics that put small business failure at 50 percent, the number of entrepreneurial ventures will only increase in the coming years. The majority of business school graduates will establish themselves through entrepreneurial efforts, either by starting their own businesses or by working with small business owners. With a number of professional organizations and the SBA devoted to small business, the new entrepreneur can find a great deal of technical, financial, and emotional support. Home-based businesses in particular are growing at a rapid rate, aided in part by the Internet. It is estimated that 20 percent of all small businesses are home based.

The Internet has been a great help to entrepreneurs. Not only has the Internet allowed them to promote their businesses internationally, it has provided great new job prospects, including information brokers, Internet consultants, and Internet entrepreneurs. As the Internet expands and develops, more people will market their wares and talents online. The Internet isn't the only opportunity for new entrepreneurs: New trends and habits have inspired such enterprises as personal chef services, medical billing companies, and personal training services.

Faced with corporate downsizing in the 1990s, more people began to reexamine their roles in the workplace. Today, people don't just want jobs—they want fulfilling careers that are both financially and emotionally rewarding. They also want time for the other aspects of their lives, such as families, hobbies, and traveling. Home-based and small business can offer these things, but not all such endeavors turn out as planned. While some would-be entrepreneurs with failed businesses return to the corporate world, others try and try again with different entrepreneurships, which is another part of the appeal of this type of business.

Each article in this book discusses a particular entrepreneurial career in detail. The articles in *Careers in Focus: Entrepreneurs* appear in Ferguson's *Encyclopedia of Careers and Vocational Guidance,* but have been updated and revised with the latest information from the U.S. Department of Labor, professional organizations, and other sources.

The following paragraphs detail the sections and features that appear in the book.

The **Quick Facts** section provides a brief summary of the career including recommended school subjects, personal skills, work environment, minimum educational requirements, salary ranges, certification or licensing requirements, and employment outlook. This section also provides acronyms and identification numbers for the following government classification indexes: the Dictionary of Occupational Titles (DOT), the Guide for Occupational Exploration (GOE), the National Occupational Classification (NOC) Index, and the Occupational Information Network (O*NET)-Standard Occupational Classification System (SOC) index. The DOT, GOE, and O*NET-SOC indexes have been created by the U.S. government; the NOC index is Canada's career classification system. Readers can use the identification numbers listed in the Quick Facts section to access further information about a career. Print editions of the DOT (*Dictionary of Occupational Titles.* Indianapolis, Ind.: JIST Works, 1991) and GOE (*Guide for Occupational Exploration.* Indianapolis, Ind.: JIST Works, 2001) are available at libraries. Electronic versions of the NOC (http://www23.hrdc-drhc.gc.ca) and O*NET-SOC (http://online.onetcenter.org) are available on the Internet. When no DOT, GOE, NOC, or O*NET-SOC numbers are present, this means that the U.S. Department of Labor or Human Resources Development Canada have not created a numerical designation for this career. In this instance, you will see the acronym "N/A," or not available.

The Overview section is a brief introductory description of the duties and responsibilities involved in this career. Oftentimes, a career may have a variety of job titles. When this is the case, alternative career titles are presented. Employment statistics are also provided, when available. The History section describes the history of the particular job as it relates to the overall development of its industry or field. The Job describes the primary and secondary duties of the job. Requirements discusses high school and postsecondary education and training requirements, any certification or licensing that is necessary, and other personal requirements for success in the job. Exploring offers suggestions on how to gain experience in or knowledge of the particular job before making a firm educational and financial commitment. The focus is on what can be done while still in high school (or in the early years of college) to gain a better understanding of the job. The Employers section gives an overview of typical places of employment for the job. Starting Out discusses the best ways to land that first job, be it through the college career services office, newspaper ads, Internet employment sites, or personal contact. The Advancement section describes what kind of career path to expect from the job and how to get there. Earnings lists salary ranges and describes the typical fringe benefits. The Work Environment section describes the typical surroundings and conditions of employment—whether indoors or outdoors, noisy or quiet, social or independent. Also discussed are typical hours worked, any seasonal fluctuations, and the stresses and strains of the job. The Outlook section summarizes the job in terms of the general economy and industry projections. For the most part, Outlook information is obtained from the U.S. Bureau of Labor Statistics and is supplemented by information gathered from professional associations. Job growth terms follow those used in the *Occupational Outlook Handbook*. Growth described as "much faster than the average" means an increase of 21 percent or more. Growth described as "faster than the average" means an increase of 14 to 20 percent. Growth described as "about as fast as the average" means an increase of 7 to 13 percent. Growth described as "more slowly than the average" means an increase of 3 to 6 percent. "Little or no change" means a decrease of 2 percent to an increase of 2 percent. "Decline" means a decrease of 3 percent or more. Each article ends with For More Information, which lists organizations that provide information on training, education, internships, scholarships, and job placement.

Careers in Focus: Entrepreneurs also includes photographs, informative sidebars, and interviews with professionals in the field.

If taking risks and working as your own boss appeal to you, then you may find a rewarding future in one of the entrepreneurial careers outlined in this book. Read each article and contact the organizations listed for more information on the areas that interest you. Although there are certain aspects of any business that are out of your control, your potential success as an entrepreneur will be limited only by your innovation and drive to succeed.

Antiques and Art Dealers

OVERVIEW

Antiques and art dealers make a living acquiring, displaying, and selling antiques and art. By strict definition, antiques are often described as items more than 100 years old. However, over the last two decades, the term "antique" has been applied to furniture, jewelry, clothing, art, household goods, and many other collectibles, dating back to as recently as the 1970s. People collect a wide array of items, from traditional paintings and sculptures to unique period toys and cigar boxes. Many antiques and art dealers are self-employed and go into business after discovering an interest in collecting pieces themselves. The Antiques and Collectibles National Association (ACNA) estimates there are approximately 200,000 to 250,000 antique dealers in the United States, based in antique shops, antique malls, and on the Internet.

HISTORY

Interest in collecting antiques and art can be traced back to the Renaissance, when people began to admire and prize Greek and Roman antiquities such as coins, manuscripts, sculptures, paintings, and pieces of architecture. To fulfill public interest and curiosity, as well as to supply the growing number of private and public collections, many pieces from Egypt, Italy, and Greece were looted and carried off to other countries.

The collectibles market, as it is known today, consists of everyday household objects, as well as furniture, clothing, art, and even

QUICK FACTS

School Subjects
Art
Art history
Business
Family and consumer science

Personal Skills
Artistic
Leadership/management

Work Environment
Primarily indoors
Primarily multiple locations

Minimum Education Level
High school diploma

Salary Range
$15,000 to $30,000 to $1 million

Certification or Licensing
None available

Outlook
About as fast as the average

DOT
N/A

GOE
N/A

NOC
0621

O*NET-SOC
N/A

automobiles, usually originating from another time period. After World War I, interest in collectibles grew. Many people began to purchase, preserve, and display pieces in their homes. As interest grew, so did the need for antiques and art businesses and dealers.

There are different categories of collectibles and different ways and reasons to acquire them. Some people choose to collect pieces from different time periods such as American Colonial or Victorian; others collect by the pattern or brand, such as Chippendale furniture or Coca-Cola memorabilia. Some people collect objects related to their career or business. For example, a physician may collect early surgical instruments, while a pharmacist may be interested in antique apothecary cabinets. A growing category in the collectibles industry is ephemera. Ephemera include theater programs, postcards, cigarette cards, and food labels, among others. These items were produced without lasting value or survival in mind. Though many pieces of ephemera can be purchased inexpensively, others, especially items among the first of their kind or in excellent condition, are rare and considered very valuable.

Some larger antiques and art dealers specialize and deal only with items from a particular time period or design. However, most dealers collect, buy, and sell all kinds of previously owned household items and decor. Such shops will carry items ranging from dining room furniture to jewelry to cooking molds.

The idea of what is worth collecting constantly changes with time and the public's tastes and interests. Art tastes range from traditional to contemporary, from Picasso to Warhol. Items representing the rock music industry of the 1960s and 1970s, as well as household items and furniture of the 1970s, are highly sought after today. Dealers not only stock their stores with items currently in demand but keep an eye on the collectibles of the future.

THE JOB

For Sandra Naujokas, proprietor of Favorite Things Antique Shop, in Orland Park, Illinois, the antiques business is never boring. More than 25 years ago, she started a collection of English-style china, and she's been hooked on antiques and collecting ever since. Naujokas spends her workday greeting customers and answering any questions they may have. When business slows down, she cleans the store and prices inventory. Sometimes people will bring in items for resale. It's up to Naujokas to carefully inspect each piece and settle on a price. She relies on pricing manuals such as *Kovels' Antiques & Collectibles Price List* and *Schroeder's Antiques Price*

Guide, which give guidelines and a suggested price on a wide range of items.

Naujokas also goes on a number of shopping expeditions every year to restock her store. Besides rummage sales and auctions, she relies on buying trips to different parts of the country and abroad to find regional items. At times, she is invited to a person's home to view items for sale. "It's important to be open to all possibilities," Naujokas says.

She also participates in several shows a year to reach customers who normally would not travel to the store's location. "You need to do a variety of things to advertise your wares," Naujokas advises.

She also promotes her business by advertising in her town's travel brochure, the local newspapers, and by direct mail campaigns. Her schedule is grueling, as the store is open seven days a week, but Naujokas enjoys the work and the challenge of being an antique dealer. Besides the social aspect—interacting with all sorts of people and situations—Naujokas loves having the first choice of items for her personal collections. Her advice for people interested in having their own antique store? "You have to really like the items you intend to sell."

REQUIREMENTS

High School

You can become an antiques or art dealer with a high school diploma, though many successful dealers have become specialists in their field partly through further education. While in high school, concentrate on history and art classes to familiarize yourself with the particular significance and details of different periods in time and the corresponding art of the period. Consider studying home economics if you plan to specialize in household items. This knowledge can come in handy when distinguishing a wooden rolling pin from a wooden butter paddle, for example.

English and speech classes to improve communication skills are also helpful. Antiques and art dealing is a people-oriented business. For this reason, it's crucial to be able to deal efficiently with different types of people and situations. Operating your own small business will also require skills such as accounting, simple bookkeeping, and marketing, so business classes are recommended.

Postsecondary Training

While a college education is not required, a degree in fine arts, art history, or history will give you a working knowledge of the antiques you sell and the historical periods from which they originated. Another option is obtaining a degree in business or entrepreneurship. Such knowledge will help you to run a successful business.

Certification or Licensing

Presently, there are no certification programs available for antiques dealers. However, if you plan to open your own antique store, you will need a local business license or permit.

In addition, if you wish to conduct appraisals, it will be necessary to take appraisal courses that are appropriate for your interest or antique specialty. Certification is not required of those interested in working as an appraiser, but it is highly recommended, according to the International Society of Appraisers (ISA)—which administers an accreditation and certification program to its members. Obtaining accreditation or certification will demonstrate your knowledge and expertise in appraisal and attract customers. To obtain accreditation, candidates must have three years of experience in appraising, complete the ISA Core Course in Appraisal Studies, and pass an examination. To become certified, individuals must complete additional training in their specialty area, submit two appraisals for peer review, complete professional development study, and pass a comprehensive examination.

Other Requirements

To be an antiques or art dealer, you'll need patience—and lots of it. Keeping your store well stocked with antiques, art, or other collectibles takes numerous buying trips to auctions, estate sales, flea markets, rummage sales, and even to foreign countries. Many times you'll have to sort through boxes of ordinary "stuff" before coming across a treasure. Unless you're lucky enough to have a large staff, you will have to make these outings by yourself. However, most dealers go into the profession because they enjoy the challenge of hunting for valuable pieces.

In addition to being patient in the hunt for treasure, art dealers also have to be patient when dealing with clients. Works of art can cost thousands, even millions of dollars; as a result, purchases are typically not quick decisions. The ability to work with a client over some time and gradually persuade them to invest in a piece takes time, skill, patience and tact.

Tact is another must-have quality for success in this industry. Remember the old adage—one person's trash is another person's treasure.

Finally, with the growth of online auction sites such as eBay, computer skills have come to be an essential part of the antique or collectible dealer's toolkit.

EXPLORING

To explore this field further, you may want to start by visiting an antique store or art gallery. If you see valuable treasures as opposed to dull paintings, old furniture, outdated books, or dusty collectibles, then chances are this is the job for you.

You can also tune to an episode of public television's traveling antique show, *Antiques Roadshow* (http://www.pbs.org/wgbh/pages/roadshow), where people are encouraged to bring family treasures or rummage sale bargains for appraisal by antique industry experts.

EMPLOYERS

Many antiques and art dealers and are self-employed, operating their own shops or renting space at a local mall. Others operate solely through traveling art shows or through mail-order catalogues. Some dealers prefer to work as employees of larger antique or art galleries. In general, the more well known the dealer, the more permanent and steady the business. Prestigious auction houses such as Christie's or Sotheby's are attractive places to work, but competition for such jobs is fierce.

STARTING OUT

All dealers have a great interest in antiques or art and are collectors themselves. Often, their businesses result from an overabundance of their personal collections. There are many ways to build your collection and create inventory worthy of an antique business. Attending yard sales is an inexpensive way to build your inventory; you'll never know what kind of valuables you will come across. Flea markets, local art galleries, and antique malls will provide great purchasing opportunities and give you the chance to check out the competition. Sandra Naujokas finds that spring is an especially busy time for collecting. As people do their "spring cleaning," many decide to part with household items and décor they no longer want or need.

ADVANCEMENT

For those working out of their homes or renting showcase space at malls or larger shops, advancement in this field can mean opening your own antique shop or art gallery. Besides a business license, dealers who open their own stores need to apply for a seller's permit and a state tax identification number.

At this point, advancement is based on the success of the business. To ensure that their business thrives and expands, dealers need to develop advertising and marketing ideas to keep their business in the public's eye. Besides using the local library or Internet for ideas on opening their own businesses, newer dealers often turn to people who are already in the antiques and art business for valuable advice.

EARNINGS

It is difficult to gauge what antiques and art dealers earn because of the vastness of the industry. Some internationally known, high-end antique stores and art galleries dealing with many pieces of priceless furniture or works of art may make millions of dollars in yearly profits. This, however, is the exception. It is impossible to compare the high-end dealer with the lower end market. The majority of antiques and art dealers are comparatively small in size and type of inventory. Some dealers work only part time or rent showcase space from established shops.

According to a survey conducted by the ACNA, the average showcase dealer earns about $1,000 a month in gross profits. From there, each dealer earns a net profit as determined by the piece or pieces sold, after overhead and other business costs. Annual earnings vary greatly for antiques and art dealers due to factors such as size and specialization of the store, location, the market, and current trends and tastes of the public.

WORK ENVIRONMENT

Much of antiques and art dealers' time is spent indoors. Many smaller antique shops and art galleries do not operate with a large staff, so dealers must be prepared to work alone at times. Also, there may be large gaps of time between customers. Most stores are open at least five days a week and operate during regular business hours, though some have extended shopping hours in the evening.

However, dealers are not always stuck in their store. Buying trips and shopping expeditions give them opportunities to restock their inventory, not to mention explore different regions of the country or world. Naujokas finds that spring is the busiest time for building her store's merchandise, while the holiday season is a busy selling time.

OUTLOOK

According to the ACNA, the collectibles industry should enjoy moderate growth in future years. The Internet has quickly become a popular way to buy and sell antiques and art. Though this medium has introduced collecting to many people worldwide, it has also had an adverse affect on the industry, namely for dealers and businesses that sell antiques and art in more traditional settings such as a shop or mall, or at a trade show. However, some industry experts predict that the popularity of Web sites devoted to selling collectibles will level off. There is a great social aspect to collecting art and antiques. They believe that people want to see, feel, and touch the items they are interested in purchasing, which is obviously not possible to do while surfing the Web.

Although the number of authentic antique art and collectibles—items more than 100 years old—is limited, new items will be in vogue as collectibles. Also, people will be ready to sell old furniture and other belongings to make room for new, modern purchases. It is unlikely that there will ever be a shortage of inventory worthy of an antique shop or art gallery.

FOR MORE INFORMATION

For industry information, antique show schedules, and appraisal information, contact
Antiques and Collectibles National Association (ACNA)
PO Box 4389
Davidson, NC 28036-4389
Tel: 800-287-7127
http://www.antiqueandcollectible.com

For art resources and listings of galleries, contact
Art Dealers Association of America
205 Lexington Avenue, Suite #901
New York, NY 10016-6022
Tel: 212-488-5550
http://www.artdealers.org

Contact the FADA for information on art galleries nationwide and special events.
Fine Art Dealers Association (FADA)
PO Box D-1
Carmel, CA 93921-0729
http://www.fada.com

For information about appraising and certification, contact
International Society of Appraisers
230 East Ohio Street, Suite 400
Chicago, IL 60611-3645
Tel: 312-224-2567
Email: isa@isa-appraisers.org
http://www.isa-appraisers.org

For programming schedules and tour information on the public television show that highlights unique and sometimes priceless antique finds, visit
Antiques Roadshow
http://www.pbs.org/wgbh/pages/roadshow

For information on collecting, art and antique shows, and collecting clubs, visit
Collectors.org
http://www.collectors.org

Bed and Breakfast Owners

OVERVIEW

A bed and breakfast is an inn, or small hotel, of about four to 20 rooms. *Bed and breakfast owners,* either single-handedly or with the help of spouse and family, provide guests with a comfortable, home-like environment. These workers, sometimes called *innkeepers* or abbreviated to *B & B owners,* clean rooms, provide guests with rooms, keep books and records, and provide some meals. They also provide information about tours, museums, restaurants, theaters, and recreational areas. There are approximately 20,000 bed and breakfasts in the country. Though a bed and breakfast may be located in the very heart of a large city, most are located in small towns, the country, and along oceans, lakes, or rivers.

HISTORY

The bed and breakfast, or "B & B" as it is affectionately known, is an example of one of the most basic and traditional forms of lodging enhanced by comfortable and charming frills. Though initially considered nothing more than a bed for weary travelers, inns became, over the centuries, clean and comfortable establishments that provided comfortable rest and good food and served as important community centers. Some of the first Elizabethan theaters were simply the courtyards of English lodges. The lodging houses of the first American colonies were styled after these English inns and were considered so necessary that a law in 18th-century Massachusetts required that towns provide roadside lodging.

QUICK FACTS

School Subjects
Business
Family and consumer science

Personal Skills
Communication/ideas
Leadership/management

Work Environment
Primarily one location
Indoors and outdoors

Minimum Education Level
High school diploma

Salary Range
$7,000 to $75,000 to
$168,000+

Certification or Licensing
Required by certain states

Outlook
About as fast as the average

DOT
N/A

GOE
N/A

NOC
0632

O*NET-SOC
N/A

These early examples of bed and breakfasts thrived for years—until the development of the railroad. Large luxury hotels popped up next to railroad stations and did a booming business. Some inns survived, but many became more like hotels in the process, adding rooms and giving less personal service. Other inns became boarding houses, renting rooms by the week and the month. When people took to the highways in automobiles, lodging changed once again, inspiring the development of motels and tourist camps. It has only been in the last 20 years or so that inns have become popular forms of lodging again, with bed and breakfasts opening up in historic houses and towns. In 1980, there were approximately 5,000 inns in the country; today, that number has more than quadrupled.

THE JOB

Have you ever wanted to vacation with a former FBI Public Enemy #1? Probably not. But in Tucson, Arizona, you can sit in the Jacuzzi of the Dillinger House Bed and Breakfast and imagine yourself to be in the company of the 1930s-era bank robber John Dillinger. Mark Muchmore now owns the house and grounds where Dillinger was captured. Though a house with such history may not seem a natural source for a bed and breakfast, the history actually gives the place a unique distinction in the area. Dillinger's respite in the desert town is part of local legend, and his capture is still celebrated with annual parties and dramatic recreations in some of Tucson's bars. One of the great appeals of bed and breakfasts are the stories behind them. Though not every bed and breakfast has a history as colorful as that of the Dillinger House, many do have well-documented backgrounds. Bed and breakfast owners therefore become great sources of local history and valuable guides to area sites.

Most of the bed and breakfasts across the country are housed in historical structures: the Victorian houses of Cape May, New Jersey, Brooklyn brownstones, and a house in Illinois designed by Frank Lloyd Wright are just a few examples. Many are furnished with antiques. Muchmore owned his house for some time before turning it into a bed and breakfast. A job change inspired him to start a new business, opening up his home to guests. "I had always wanted to do something like this," he says. "I already had the property, a large house, and two adjacent guest houses, so it seemed perfect."

As the name "bed and breakfast" suggests, a good homemade breakfast is an essential part of any inn stay. Muchmore's day starts much earlier than Dillinger's ever did and is likely much more serene; he's typically up at 5:00 A.M. grinding coffee beans, harvesting herbs, and preparing to bake. "I accommodate any and all dietary restrictions," Muchmore says, "and do it in such a way that my guests feel the attention and respect." After serving his guests their breakfast and cleaning up, Muchmore sees to business concerns such as answering email messages, calling prospective guests, and taking reservations. Once the guests have left their rooms, Muchmore can clean the rooms and do some laundry. After grocery shopping, he returns to his office for book work and to prepare brochures for the mail.

Among all the daily tasks, Muchmore reserves time to get to know his guests and to make sure they're enjoying their stay. "I like interacting with my guests," he says. "I like hearing about their jobs, their lives, their likes and dislikes. I love to be able to give them sightseeing suggestions, restaurant tips, and from time to time, little extras like a bowl of fresh citrus from my trees." It is such close attention to detail that makes a bed and breakfast successful. The guests of bed and breakfasts are looking for more personal attention and warmer hospitality than they'd receive from a large hotel chain.

Though the owners of bed and breakfasts are giving up much of their privacy by allowing guests to stay in the rooms of their own homes, they do have their houses to themselves from time to time. Some bed and breakfasts are only open during peak tourist season, and some are only open on weekends. And even those open year-round may often be without guests. For some owners, inconsistency in the business is not a problem; many bed and breakfasts are owned by couples and serve as a second income. While one person works at another job, the other tends to the needs of the bed and breakfast.

The Professional Association of Innkeepers International (PAII), a professional association for the owners of bed and breakfasts and country inns, classifies the different kinds of bed and breakfasts. A host home is considered a very small business with only a few rooms for rent. Because of its small size, the owner of a host home may not be required by law to license the business or to have government inspections. Without advertising or signs, guests primarily find these homes through reservation service organizations. A bed and breakfast and bed and breakfast inn are classified as having four or more rooms. They adhere to license, inspection, and zoning requirements and promote their businesses through brochures, print ads, and signs. A country inn is considered a bit larger, with 10 or more rooms, and it may serve one meal in addition to breakfast.

REQUIREMENTS
High School
Because you'll essentially be maintaining a home as a bed and breakfast owner, you should take home economics courses. These courses

can prepare you for the requirements of shopping and cooking for a group of people, as well as budgeting household finances. But a bed and breakfast is also a business, so you need to further develop those budgeting skills in a business fundamentals class, accounting, and math. A shop class, or some other hands-on workshop, can be very valuable to you; take a class that will teach you about electrical wiring, woodworking, and other elements of home repair.

Postsecondary Training

As a bed and breakfast owner, you're in business for yourself, so there are no educational requirements for success. Also, no one specific degree program will better prepare you than any other. A degree in history or art may be as valuable as a degree in business management. Before taking over a bed and breakfast, though, you may consider enrolling in a hotel management or small business program at your local community college. Such programs can educate you in the practical aspects of running a bed and breakfast, from finances and loans to health and licensing regulations.

Opportunities for part-time jobs and internships with a bed and breakfast are few and far between. Bed and breakfast owners can usually use extra help during busy seasons, but can't always afford to hire a staff. But some do enough business that they can hire a housekeeper or a secretary, or they may have an extra room to provide for an apprentice willing to help with the business.

Certification or Licensing

Though bed and breakfast owners generally aren't certified or licensed as individuals, they do license their businesses and seek accreditation for their inns from professional organizations such as PAII. With accreditation, the business can receive referrals from the associations and can be included in their directories. A house with only a room or two for rent may not be subject to any licensing requirements, but most bed and breakfasts are state regulated. A bed and breakfast owner must follow zoning regulations, maintain a small business license, pass health inspections, and carry sufficient liability insurance.

Other Requirements

Bed and breakfast ownership requires diverse skills. You must have a head for business, but you have to be comfortable working among people outside of an office. You must be creative in the way you maintain the house, paying attention to decor and gardening, but you should also have practical skills in plumbing and other household repair (or you should at least be capable of diagnosing any need

U.S. Bed and Breakfast Industry, 2006

- There were approximately 20,000 bed and breakfasts, with an average of 7.66 rooms per inn.
- A total of 153,200 rooms were available to customers.
- The average occupancy rate was 43 percent—an increase of 5 percent from 2002.
- The average daily rate was $166—an increase of $29.30 from 2002. Daily room rates ranged from $40 to $875.
- 82 percent of bed and breakfast owners were couples.
- 88 percent of owners lived on B & B premises.

Source: Professional Association of Innkeepers International

for repair). A knowledge of the electrical wiring of your house and the phone lines is valuable. You'll also need an ability to cook well for groups both large and small.

"I'm easygoing," Mark Muchmore says in regard to how he makes his business a success, "and I know how to set, and follow through on, personal and professional goals. I'm also a natural organizer, and pay attention to details." Muchmore also enjoys meeting new people, which is very important. You'll be expected to be a gracious host to all your guests. But you'll also have to maintain rules and regulations; guests of bed and breakfasts expect a quiet environment, and smoking and drinking is often prohibited.

If turning your home into a bed and breakfast, you should learn about city planning and zoning restrictions, as well as inspection programs. Computer skills will help you to better organize reservations, registration histories, and tax records. You should have some knowledge of marketing in order to promote your business by ads, brochures, and on the Internet.

EXPLORING

The PAII provides students with a free informational packet about innkeeping and puts together an "Aspiring Innkeeper Kit" for those interested in the requirements of running a bed and breakfast. It also publishes a newsletter and books on innkeeping, holds conferences, and maintains a very informative Web site (http://www.paii.org). If there are inns in your town, interview the owners and spend a day or two with them as they perform their daily duties. The owner may even have part-time positions open for someone to assist with preparing breakfast or cleaning the rooms—employment of staff has increased in the last few years. Some bed and breakfast owners occasionally hire reliable "innsitters" to manage their inns when they're out of town.

Even a job as a motel housekeeper or desk clerk can give you experience with the responsibilities of innkeeping. Bed and breakfasts, hotels, and resorts across the country often advertise nationally for seasonal assistance. For years, high school and college students have made a little extra money working in exotic locales by dedicating their summers to full-time hotel or resort jobs. Wait staff, poolside assistants, kitchen staff, housekeepers, and spa assistants are needed in abundance during peak tourist seasons. In some cases, you can get a paid position, and in others you may be expected to work in exchange for room and board. Even if your summer job is at a large resort rather than a small bed and breakfast, you can still develop valuable people skills and learn a lot about the travel and tourism industry.

EMPLOYERS

Innkeepers work for themselves. The charm of bed and breakfasts is that they are owned and operated by individuals, or individual families, who live on the premises. Though bed and breakfast "chains" may be a thing of the future, they are not expected to greatly affect the business of the traditional "mom and pop" operations.

Most bed and breakfasts exist in rural areas and small towns where there are no large hotels. Though the number of inns in cities is increasing, only 12 percent of the inns in the United States are located in urban areas. According to the PAII, the majority of inns (54 percent) are in small resort villages. Twenty-nine percent of the inns are in rural areas.

An innkeeper's income is derived from room rental and fees for any "extras" such as additional meals and transportation. An inn's guests are often from outside of the local area, but an inn may also cater to many area residents. Most guests are screened by reservation service organizations or travel associations; this helps to protect both the guest and the owner. Bed and breakfasts must pass certain approval requirements, and guests must prove to be reliable, paying customers.

STARTING OUT

Probably all the bed and breakfast owners you speak to will have different stories about how they came to own their businesses. Some, like Mark Muchmore, convert their own homes into inns; others buy fully established businesses, complete with client lists, marketing plans, and furnishings. Others inherit their bed and breakfasts from family members, and still others lease a house from another owner. Usually, bed and breakfast ownership requires a large investment, both in time and money. Before starting your business, you must do a great deal of research. Make sure the local market can support an additional bed and breakfast and that your house and grounds will offer a unique and attractive alternative to the other lodging in the area. Research how much you can expect to make the first few years, and how much you can afford to lose. Muchmore suggests that you be sure to promote your business, but don't go overboard. "All advertising is not worth it," he says. "I have found that small ads in local publications, one listing in a nationally distributed magazine, a home or Web page, and word-of-mouth are more than enough."

Established bed and breakfasts for sale are advertised nationally, and by innkeeper associations. Prices range from under $100,000 to more than $1,000,000. An established business is often completely restored and includes antique furniture and fixtures, as well as necessary equipment.

ADVANCEMENT

Mark Muchmore sees expansion in the future of the Dillinger House Bed and Breakfast. "I see buying another property in the neighborhood," he says, "and at that point operating as an inn/spa. This would enable me to hire a small staff and include some of the extras for my guests to make them feel even more pampered." With the free time that a staff would provide, Muchmore could dedicate more time to marketing and promotion.

In many cases, a married bed and breakfast owner may continue to work full time outside of the home, while his or her spouse sees to the daily concerns of the inn. But once a business is well established with a steady clientele, both spouses may be able to commit full time to the bed and breakfast.

EARNINGS

Large, well-established bed and breakfasts can bring in tens of thousands of dollars every year, but most owners of average-sized inns must make do with much less. A survey by the PAII provides a variety of income figures. A beginning bed and breakfast has an annual net operating income of $25,000, while one seven years or older has an average income of over $73,000. A small bed and breakfast with four rooms or fewer for rent has an annual net income of about $7,000; an inn of five to eight rooms has an income of $35,000; nine to 12 rooms, $80,000. An inn with 13 to 20 rooms has a net operating income of over $168,000.

Bed and breakfasts in the western part of the United States make more money than those in other parts of the country. An average net income of $68,000 per year is figured for inns in the West, followed by $58,000 for those in the Northeast, $38,000 in the Southeast, and $33,000 in the Midwest. According to PAII, bed and breakfasts charge from $38 to $595 per day, depending on size of the room and whether it has a private bath, fireplace, and other amenities.

Bed and breakfast owners must provide their own benefits, such as health and life insurance and a savings and pension plan.

WORK ENVIRONMENT

Though working in a beautiful home with people from all around the world may sound like an ideal environment, and it may not seem like you're at work, bed and breakfast owners must perform many responsibilities to keep their property nice and pleasant. Their chores will mostly be domestic ones, keeping them close to the house with cooking, cleaning, gardening, and laundering. This makes for a very comfortable work environment over which they have a great deal of control. Though bed and breakfast owners work in their own home, they must sacrifice much of their privacy to operate their business. They must be available to their guests at all times to ensure that their stay is comfortable. However, even the most successful bed and breakfast isn't always full to capacity, and many are only open on weekends—this may result in a few long work days, then a few days of downtime. But to keep their business afloat, bed and breakfast owners will need to welcome as many guests as they can handle.

OUTLOOK

Some bed and breakfasts have been in business for decades, but it's only been in the last 20 years that inns have become popular vacation spots. PAII estimates the number of inns in the country to be approximately 20,000, up from a measly 5,000 in 1980. Tourists are seeking out inns as inexpensive and charming alternatives to the rising cost and sterile, cookie-cutter design of hotels and motels. People are even centering their vacation plans on bed and breakfasts, booking trips to historical towns for restful departures from cities.

As long as bed and breakfasts can keep their rates lower than hotel chains, they are likely to flourish.

Recognizing the appeal of bed and breakfasts, some hotel chains are considering plans to capitalize on the trend with "inn-style" lodging. An inn-style hotel is even on its way to Disneyland. Smaller hotels composed of larger, suite-style rooms with more personalized service may threaten the business of some bed and breakfasts. But the charm and historic significance of an old house can't easily be reproduced, so bed and breakfasts are expected to maintain their niche in the tourism industry.

The Americans with Disabilities Act (ADA) will also have some effect on the future of bed and breakfasts. Inns with more than six rooms are required to comply with the ADA, making their rooms and grounds handicapped accessible. When purchasing a property for the purpose of a bed and breakfast, buyers must take into consideration the expense and impact of making such additions and changes. Though some businesses may have trouble complying, those that can will open up an area of tourism previously unavailable to people with disabilities.

FOR MORE INFORMATION

To explore the bed and breakfasts of New England, contact
New England Inns & Resorts Association
PO Box 1089
44 Lafayette Road, Unit 6
North Hampton, NH 03862-1089
Tel: 603-964-6689
Email: info@neia.com
http://www.newenglandinnsandresorts.com

Contact PAII to request its free student packet, which includes information about innkeepers and their guests, seminars and consultants, and average operating expenses and revenues.
Professional Association of Innkeepers International (PAII)
207 White Horse Pike
Haddon Heights, NJ 08035-1703
Tel: 800-468-7244
Email: info@paii.org
http://www.paii.org

Caterers

QUICK FACTS

School Subjects
Business
Family and consumer science

Personal Skills
Artistic
Helping/teaching

Work Environment
Primarily indoors
Primarily multiple locations

Minimum Education Level
Some postsecondary training

Salary Range
$15,000 to $35,000 to
$75,000+

Certification or Licensing
Voluntary (certification)
Required by certain states
(licensing)

Outlook
More slowly than the average

DOT
319

GOE
09.05.02

NOC
N/A

O*NET-SOC
N/A

OVERVIEW

Caterers plan, coordinate, and supervise food service at parties and at other social functions. Working with their clients, they purchase appropriate supplies, plan menus, supervise food preparation, direct serving of food and refreshments, and ensure the overall smooth functioning of the event. As entrepreneurs, they are also responsible for budgeting, bookkeeping, and other administrative tasks.

HISTORY

Catering is part of the food service industry and has been around for as long as there have been restaurants. Once viewed as a service available only to the very wealthy, catering today is used by many people for various types of gatherings.

THE JOB

A caterer is a chef, purchasing agent, personnel director, and accountant. Often a caterer will also play the role of host, allowing clients to enjoy their own party. A caterer's responsibilities vary, depending on the size of the catering firm and the specific needs of individual clients. While preparing quality food is a concern no matter what the size of the party, larger events require far more planning and coordination. For example, a large catering firm may organize and plan a formal event for 1,000 people, including planning and preparing a seven-course meal, decorating the hall with flowers and wall hangings, employing 20 or more wait staff to serve food, and arranging the entertainment. The catering firm will also set up the tables and

22

chairs and provide the necessary linen, silverware, and dishes. A catering company may organize 50 or so such events a month or only several a year. A smaller catering organization may concentrate on simpler events, such as preparing food for an informal buffet for 15 people.

Caterers service not only individual clients but also industrial clients. A caterer may supervise a company cafeteria or plan food service for an airline or cruise ship. Such caterers often take over full-time supervision of food operations, including ordering food and other supplies, supervising personnel and food preparation, and overseeing the maintenance of equipment.

Caterers need to be flexible in their approach to food preparation, that is, able to prepare food both on- and off-premises, as required by logistical considerations and the wishes of the client. For example, if the caterer is handling a large banquet in a hotel or other location, he or she will usually prepare the food on-premises, using kitchen and storage facilities as needed. The caterer might also work in a client's kitchen for an event in a private home. In both cases, the caterer must visit the site of the function well before the actual event to determine how and where the food will be prepared. Caterers may also prepare food off-premises, working either in their own kitchens or in a mobile kitchen.

Working with the client is obviously a very important aspect of the caterer's job. Clients always want their affairs to be extra special, and the caterer's ability to present such items as a uniquely shaped wedding cake or to provide beautiful decorations will enhance the ambiance and contribute to customer satisfaction. The caterer and the client work together to establish a budget, develop a menu, and determine the desired atmosphere. Many caterers have their own special recipes, and they are always on the lookout for quality fruits, vegetables, and meats. Caterers should have an eye for detail and be able to make fancy hors d'oeuvres and eye-catching fruit and vegetable displays.

Although caterers can usually prepare a variety of dishes, they may have a specialty, such as Cajun or Italian cuisine. Caterers may also have a unique serving style (for example, serving food in Renaissance period dress) that sets them apart from other caterers. Developing a reputation by specializing in a certain area is a particularly effective marketing technique.

The caterer is a coordinator who works with suppliers, food servers, and the client to ensure that an event comes off as planned. The caterer must be in frequent contact with all parties involved in the affair, making sure, for example, that the food is delivered on time, the flowers are fresh, and the entertainment shows up and performs as promised.

Good management skills are extremely important. The caterer must know how much food and other supplies to order, what equipment will be needed, how many staff to hire, and how to coordinate various activities to ensure a smooth-running event. Purchasing the proper supplies entails knowledge of a variety of food products, their suppliers, and the contacts needed to get the right product at the best possible price.

Caterers working in a large operation may appoint a manager to oversee an event. The manager will take care of the ordering, planning, and supervising responsibilities and may even work with the client.

As entrepreneurs, caterers have many important day-to-day administrative responsibilities, such as overseeing the budgeting and bookkeeping of the operation. They must make sure that the business continues to make a profit while keeping its prices competitive. Additionally, caterers must know how to figure costs and other budgetary considerations, plan inventories, buy food, and ensure compliance with health regulations.

Caterer helpers may prepare and serve hors d'oeuvres and other food and refreshments at social functions under the supervision of the head caterer. They also help arrange tables and decorations and then assist in the cleanup.

REQUIREMENTS
High School
Does working as a caterer sound interesting to you? If so, you should take home economics or family and consumer science classes in high school. Any class that will teach you about food preparation, presentation, and nutrition will be valuable. Since caterers run their own businesses, you should also take math, accounting and bookkeeping, and business classes to prepare for dealing with budgets, record keeping, and management. Like so many small business owners today, most caterers will use computers for such things as planning schedules, keeping addresses, and updating accounts, so be sure to take computer classes. English classes will help you to hone your communication skills, which will be essential when you deal with customers. Finally, round out your education by taking health and science classes, which will give you an added understanding of nutrition, how the body works, and how to prevent food contamination.

Postsecondary Training

The best way to enter the catering industry is through a formal training program. One way of obtaining this education is to attend a vocational or community college with an appropriate program. Many of these schools and colleges offer professional training in food science, food preparation, and catering. Often these programs will provide opportunities for students to work in apprentice positions to gain hands-on experience.

As the catering field has grown more competitive, many successful caterers are now choosing to get a college degree in business administration, family and consumer science (home economics), nutrition, or a related field. If you decide to get a four-year college degree, make sure your course work includes subjects in nutrition, health, and business management, regardless of your major. A number of colleges and universities also offer assistance to their students in finding apprenticeships. The Foundation of the National Association of Catering Executives (NACE) provides information on universities and colleges offering programs relevant to those interested in the catering profession.

Certification or Licensing

As a measure of professional status, many caterers become certified through the NACE. To qualify for this certification, called the certified professional catering executive, caterers must meet certain educational and professional requirements as well as pass a written examination. To keep their certification current, caterers must also fulfill requirements such as completing continuing education courses and attending professional conferences. The International Food Service Executives Association also offers the certified food executive, the certified food manager, and other certification designations. Applications are available online; see the Web site listed at the end of the article for more information.

Most states require caterers to be licensed, and inspectors may make periodic visits to catering operations to ensure that local health and safety regulations are being maintained in food preparation, handling, and storage.

Other Requirements

The professional caterer should have a commitment to learning. Foods go in and out of fashion, new techniques develop, and our understanding of nutrition and health is always growing. The successful caterer will want to keep up with these new developments in the field. Because caterers run their own businesses, they should be organized, able to work on tight schedules, and conscientious about keeping accurate records. The successful caterer enjoys working with people and also has an artistic eye, with the ability to arrange food and settings in an appealing manner.

EXPLORING

One relatively simple way for you to begin exploring your interest in catering is to do some cooking at home. Make dinner for your family once a week, try out a new recipe for muffins, or bake cookies for your friends. If people enjoy your creations, you may be able to offer catering services to them when they have parties.

If your high school has a club for those interested in home economics, join it. You'll meet other people with similar interests and may find others to cook with. Some organizations, such as 4-H, offer programs about food preparation and careers in food service. Find out if there is such a group in your area and join it as well.

Another great way to explore food service is through service work. Volunteering in the kitchen of a local homeless shelter where you can help prepare meals for large numbers of people can provide a great experience, both for your professional ambitions and for humanitarian reasons.

Finally, get part-time or summer work at a local restaurant. Even if you end up working at an ice cream parlor when what you really want to do is cater eight-course meals, you'll still gain valuable experience working with food, money, and customers.

Helpful Web Site

EntrepreneurU
http://www.entrepreneurU.org

EntrepreneurU, which was created by DECA Inc. and the Ewing Marion Kauffman Foundation, is a good place to start for students interested in pursuing an entrepreneurial career. It offers an overview of entrepreneurism, details on what is taught during an entrepreneurism course, information on scholarships, and much more. Most importantly, it features a searchable database of two- and four-year entrepreneurship programs in the United States. The database is searchable by name of school, region, state, type of degree, length of program, career field the entrepreneurial program is associated with (such as business, culinary arts, engineering, medicine, tourism, etc.), and whether the program is women-focused.

EMPLOYERS

Most caterers own their own businesses and are, therefore, self-employed. Caterers, however, do have many different types of clients. Individuals may need catering services for a party or special family celebration. Industrial clients, such as company cafeterias, airlines, country clubs, schools, banquet halls, cruise ships, and hotels, may require catering services on a large scale or at regular intervals.

STARTING OUT

Some caterers enter the profession as a matter of chance after helping a friend or relative prepare a large banquet or volunteering to coordinate a group function. Most caterers, however, begin their careers after graduating from college with a degree in a program such as home economics or finishing a culinary training program at a vocational school or community college.

Qualified individuals can begin working as a manager for a large catering firm or as a manager for a hotel or country club or banquet service. Those most likely to start a catering business will have extensive experience and sufficient finances to purchase equipment and cover other start-up costs.

ADVANCEMENT

As with most service-oriented businesses, the success of a caterer depends on the quality of work and a good reputation. Well-known caterers can expand their businesses, often growing from a small business to a larger operation. This may mean hiring assistants and buying more equipment to be able to serve a larger variety of clientele. Caterers who initially worked out of their own home kitchens may get an office or relocate to another area to take advantage of better catering opportunities. Sometimes successful caterers use their skills and reputations to secure full-time positions in large hotels or restaurants as banquet coordinators and planners. Independent caterers may also secure contracts with industrial clients, such as airlines, hospitals, schools, and corporations, to staff their cafeterias or supply food and beverages. They may also be employed by such companies to manage their food operations.

EARNINGS

Earnings vary widely, depending on the size and location of the catering operation and the skill and motivation of the individual entrepreneur. Many caterers charge according to the number of guests attending a function. In many cases, the larger the event, the larger the profit. Earnings are also influenced by whether a caterer works full time or only part time. Even very successful caterers often work part time, working another job either because they enjoy it or to protect themselves against a possible downturn in the economy.

Full-time caterers can earn between $15,000 and $60,000 per year, depending on skill, reputation, and experience. An extremely successful caterer can easily earn more than $75,000 annually. A part-time caterer may earn $7,000 to $15,000 per year, subject to the same variables as the full-time caterer. Because most caterers are self-employed, vacations and other benefits are usually not part of the wage structure.

WORK ENVIRONMENT

A caterer often works long hours planning and preparing for an event, and the day of the event might easily be a 14-hour workday, from setup to cleanup. Caterers often spend long hours on their feet, and although the work can be physically and mentally demanding, they usually enjoy a great deal of work flexibility. As entrepreneurs, they can usually take time off when necessary. Caterers often work more than 60 hours a week during busy seasons, with most of the work on weekends and evenings, when events tend to be scheduled.

There is a lot of variety in the type of work a caterer does. The caterer must work closely with a variety of clients and be able to adapt to last-minute changes. Caterers must be able to plan ahead, work gracefully under pressure, and have the ability to adapt to last-minute mishaps. Attention to detail is critical, as is the ability to work long hours under demanding situations. They must be able to direct a large staff of kitchen workers and waitpersons and be able to interact well with clients, guests, and employees.

OUTLOOK

The U.S. Department of Labor projects that employment opportunities in food service will grow more slowly than the average rate through 2016. Despite this prediction, opportunities will be good for individuals who handle special events, such as weddings, bar and bat mitzvahs, and other festive occasions less affected by downswings in the economy. On the other hand, events such as business functions may offer less catering opportunities during times of recession and cutbacks.

Competition is keen as many hotels and restaurants branch out to offer catering services. However, despite competition and fluctuating economic conditions, highly skilled and motivated caterers should be in demand throughout the country, especially in and around large metropolitan areas.

FOR MORE INFORMATION

For information on scholarships, student branches, certification, and industry news, contact
International Food Service Executives Association
8155 Briar Cliff Drive
Castle Pines North, CO 80108-8215
Tel: 720-733-8001
http://www.ifsea.com

For information on certification programs and catering publications, contact
National Association of Catering Executives (NACE)
9881 Broken Land Parkway, Suite 101
Columbia, MD 21046-3015
Tel: 410-290-5410
http://www.nace.net

For more information on programs and chapters, contact
National 4-H Council
7100 Connecticut Avenue
Chevy Chase, MD 20815-4934
Tel: 301-961-2800
Email: info@fourhcouncil.edu
http://www.fourhcouncil.edu

For education information, visit the following Web site:
Foundation of the National Association of Catering Executives
http://www.nacefoundation.org

Child Care
Service Owners

QUICK FACTS

School Subjects
Business
Family and consumer science

Personal Skills
Helping/teaching
Leadership/management

Work Environment
Primarily indoors
Primarily one location

Minimum Education Level
Some postsecondary training

Salary Range
$13,930 to $37,440 to
$60,000+

Certification or Licensing
Required

Outlook
Much faster than the average

DOT
N/A

GOE
12.03.03

NOC
N/A

O*NET-SOC
39-9011.00

OVERVIEW

Child care service owners provide care for infants, toddlers, and preschool-aged children. While the parents and guardians are at work, child care providers watch the children and help them develop skills through games and activities. The child care facility may be part of the owner's home, or it may be a separate center composed of classrooms, play areas, and areas for infant care. The service owner must hire, train, and schedule child care workers, or teachers, to assist with large numbers of children. The owner must also manage the center's finances, assure that the center meets legal requirements and accreditation standards, and meet with prospective clients. Child care centers are in demand all across the country, as the majority of parents of young children have jobs outside the home. There are approximately 1.4 million child care workers in the United States. According to the National Child Care Association, there are currently about 113,000 licensed child care centers in the United States.

HISTORY

Most people probably think daytime child care is a fairly modern idea. It's true that only 17 percent of the mothers of one-year-olds were part of the labor force in 1965. That number seems small when compared to statistics from the U.S. Department of Labor—today, approximately 63 percent of mothers of children under age six are working outside the home. But child care centers were needed as far back as the 18th century. In England, factories opened nurseries to care for the workers' children, a trend that carried over to the United States in the 19th century. Of course, working conditions in factories were often terrible before the 1900s, and the children were put to work at very young ages. So the child care service as we know it today didn't really begin to evolve until World War II, when women joined the workforce while the men were off fighting. Though many of these women quit their jobs when the men returned from the war, roles for women began to change. The last half of the 20th century saw more opportunities for women in the workplace and, for many families, two incomes became necessary to meet the rising costs of living. Findings by the U.S. Census Bureau indicate that today only about 15 percent of married couples with young children have one parent working and one parent staying at home. This has put dependable, safe child care services in high demand.

THE JOB

Child care workers are responsible for taking care of several children of various ages every single workday, and owners of child care services must make sure that the care the children receive is of the highest possible quality. Parents expect those working at care centers to help their children learn basic skills, such as using a spoon and playing together, and to prepare them for their first years of school by, for example, teaching colors and letters. Service owners come up with activities that build on children's abilities and curiosity. Attention to the individual needs of each child is important, so that activities can be adapted to specific needs. For example, a three-year-old child has different motor skills and reasoning abilities than a child of five years of age, and the younger child will need more help completing the same project. Child care centers typically provide care for babies, toddlers, and children of prekindergarten age, and because of this, they offer many different kinds of instruction. Some kids will just be learning how to tie their shoes and button their coats, while others will have begun to develop reading and computer skills. And, of course, the infants require much individual attention for things such as feedings, diaper changings, and being held when awake. Owners of small facilities are typically the primary care givers and do the majority of these activities in addition to the administrative activities involved in running a business—ordering supplies, paying the bills, keeping records, making sure the center meets licensing requirements, and so forth. Owners of large facilities hire aides, teachers, and assistant directors to help provide care.

Nancy Moretti owns a child care center in Smithfield, Rhode Island, called Just For Kids. The center is licensed to care for 54 children and is composed of five classrooms—each room for a different age group. She has a staff of 18 who work with kids from six weeks to five years old. "Everyone here loves children," Moretti says. "We're an extended family; we all look out for each other." Moretti's day starts with a walk through the classrooms to make sure everything is in order and to make sure all the staff members and children are there. Much of Moretti's work consists of attending to staff concerns, such as payment and scheduling. When hiring teachers for her center, she looks for people with some background in child development, such as a college degree or some years of practical experience.

A background in child development gives owners and teachers the knowledge of how to create a flexible and age-appropriate schedule that allows time for music, art, playtime, academics, rest, and other activities. Owners and child care staff work with the youngest children to teach them the days of the week and to recognize colors, seasons, and animal names and characteristics; older children are taught number and letter recognition and simple writing skills. Self-confidence and the development of communications skills are encouraged in day care centers. For example, children may be given simple art projects, such as finger painting, and after the paintings are completed everyone takes a turn showing and explaining the finished projects to the rest of the class. Show and tell gives students opportunities to speak and listen to others. Other skills children are taught may include picking up their toys after play time and washing their hands before snack time.

Owners of both small and large facilities have many other responsibilities aside from lessons and instruction. They may need to spend a large portion of a day comforting a child, helping him or her to adjust to being away from home, and finding ways to include the child in group activities. Children who become frightened or homesick need reassurance. Children also need help with tasks, such as putting on and taking off their coats and boots in the winter. If a child becomes sick, the owner must decide how to handle the situation and may contact the child's parents, a doctor, or even a hospital. Owners also order supplies for activities and supervise events, such as snack time, during which they teach children how to eat properly and clean up after themselves.

Child care center owners also work with the parents of each child. It is not unusual for parents to come to preschool and observe a child or go on a field trip with the class, and child care workers often take these opportunities to discuss the progress of each child

The owner of a day-care center reads a story to children. *(Sarah Beth Barnett, AP Photo/Star Tribune)*

as well as any specific problems or concerns. Scheduled meetings are available for parents who cannot visit the school during the day. Moretti makes it a point to be frequently available for the parents when they're dropping off and picking up the children. "Parents need to know that I'm here," she says. "For the owner to be involved is important to the parents."

REQUIREMENTS

High School

You should take courses in early childhood development when available. Many home economics courses include units in parenting and child care. English courses will help you to develop communication skills important in dealing with children, their parents, and a child care staff. In teaching children, you should be able to draw from a wide base of education and interests, so take courses in art, music, science, and physical education. Math and accounting courses will prepare you for the bookkeeping and management requirements of running your own business.

Postsecondary Training

A college degree isn't required for you to open a day care center, but it can serve you in a variety of ways. A child development program will give you the background needed for classroom instruction, as well as for understanding the basics of child care and psychology. A college degree will also demonstrate to your clients that you have the background necessary for good child care. A college degree program should include course work in a variety of liberal arts subjects, including English, history, and science, as well as nutrition, child development, psychology of the young child, and sociology.

Certification or Licensing

Requirements for the licensing or registering of child care workers vary from state to state. You can visit the Web site of the National Child Care Information and Technical Assistance Center (http:// nccic.acf.hhs.gov), part of the Administration for Children and Families, to find out about your state's regulatory bodies and contact information. Requirements for a child care administrator, director, or owner may include having a certain amount of child care experience or education, completing a certain amount of continuing education per year, being at least 21 years of age, and having a high school diploma. Cardiopulmonary resuscitation training is also often required. National certification may not be required of child care service owners and workers in every state, but some organizations do offer it. The Council for Professional Recognition offers the Child Development Associate (CDA) National Credentialing Program. To become a CDA, you must meet competency standards and have experience in child care. There are more than 200,000 CDAs across the country. The National Child Care Association offers the national administrator credential (NAC). To receive this credential, you must complete a special 40-hour, five-day training course. (Contact information for these organizations is listed at the end of this article.)

Other Requirements

Obviously, a love for children and a concern for their care and safety are most important. Child care comes naturally to most of those who run child care services. "I can't see myself doing anything but this," Nancy Moretti says. You should be very patient and capable of teaching children in many different stages of development. Because young children look up to adults and learn through example, it is important that a child care worker be a good role model—you should treat the children with respect and kindness, while also maintaining order and control. You must also be good at communicating with the parents, capable of addressing their concerns, and keeping them informed as to their children's progress.

EXPLORING

You can gain experience in this field by volunteering at a child care center or other preschool facility. Some high schools provide internships with local preschools for students interested in working as teacher aides. Your guidance counselor can provide information on these opportunities. Summer day camps or religious schools with preschool classes also hire high school students as counselors or counselors-in-training. Take tours of child care centers of various sizes, and talk to the owners about how they started their businesses.

EMPLOYERS

According to data from the National Child Care Association, there are approximately 113,000 licensed child care centers in the United States. Child care centers are located all across the country. Those who buy an established day care facility often find that most of the clients will come along with it. For those who start their own centers, word-of-mouth, a variety of offerings, and a good reputation will draw clients. Franchising is a viable option in this industry. Child care franchising operations are among the fastest growing centers. Primrose Schools Franchising Company and Kids 'R' Kids International are two of the child care companies offering franchises.

In some cases, people work from their homes, watching only their own children and some of the children from their neighborhoods; this is usually referred to as "family child care." Quality child care is a concern of most parents, regardless of economic standing. Single working mothers are often the hardest hit with child care expenses, and federal mandates requiring states to find work for welfare recipients means even more children need daytime care outside the home. Government programs and subsidies help to provide child care services for lower income families.

STARTING OUT

At your first opportunity, you should take part-time work at a child care center to gain firsthand experience. Contact child care centers, nursery schools, Head Start programs, and other preschool facilities to learn about job opportunities. Often there are many jobs for child care workers listed in the classified sections of newspapers. The turnover rate for child care workers is high because of the low wages and long hours. "You need to make sure child care is something you want to do," Nancy Moretti says, "before starting your own center." Some owners of child care centers are not actively involved with the day-to-day running of the business; parents, however, prefer to leave their children at a center where the owner takes an active interest in each child's well-being. Moretti purchased a day care center that had been in operation for nearly 10 years, and she had worked as a teacher and director at that center for eight of them. Knowing all the parents already helped her ease into ownership without losing a single client. For those considering buying an established daycare center, Moretti recommends that they spend a few months getting to know the parents first.

ADVANCEMENT

As their child care center becomes better known in the community, and as it gains a reputation for providing quality child care, owners may advance by expanding their businesses. With enough income, owners can hire staff members to help with child care, instruction, and administrative requirements. Nancy Moretti has expanded her Just For Kids Day Care facility in a variety of ways. She put an addition onto the building to allow for a number of new services: a full-day kindergarten, a before- and after-school program, Saturday child care, and a summer day camp.

In addition to expanding offerings at one child care center, some owners choose to open more centers. Primrose Schools Franchising Company, for example, notes that 61 percent of its franchisees own two or more Primrose Schools.

EARNINGS

It is difficult to determine exact salaries for child care service owners since revenue for child care centers varies according to the number of children cared for, whether the center is owned or rented, number of staff, and other factors. A center in a city with a higher cost of living and more staffing and licensing requirements will charge more than a center in a smaller town. No matter where it is located, however, a large percentage of a child care center's earnings goes to paying the staff. In 2001, Americans spent $38 billion on licensed child care. A 2005 report by the Children's Defense Fund found that parents paid an annual average of between $4,000 and $10,000 nationwide for the full-time care for one child. Some centers charged even more, in the range of $12,000. If a center cared for 54 children (like Nancy Moretti's) and charged $4,000 per child, the center's annual budget would be $216,000. Although this sounds like a fair amount of money, keep in mind that staff salaries must come out of this amount, and these usually account for 60 percent to 70 percent of expenses.

Sixty percent of $216,000 is $129,600, which leaves the owner with $86,400 to pay for all other expenses, such as any rent or mortgage on the center, any maintenance expenses, any food served, liability insurance premiums, and other equipment or items that are needed, such as playground equipment, paper cups, or books. After all such expenses are paid, owners can then draw their salaries.

According to the Center for the Child Care Workforce, average starting salaries for child care center directors in the early 2000s ranged from $15,808 to $37,440. Average salaries for center directors ranged from approximately $27,000 to $52,000. The U.S. Department of Labor reports the median earnings for all child care workers were $8.82 per hour in 2007. Someone working at this rate for 40 hours a week year-round would have an annual income of approximately $18,350. The department also reports the lowest paid 10 percent of child care workers earned less than $6.70 per hour (approximately $13,930 annually), and the highest paid 10 percent earned more than $13.56 per hour (approximately $28,210 annually). A child care center owner just starting out in the business and working as the only employee may have earnings comparable to that of the average child care worker. An experienced child care service owner running a large and well-established center, on the other hand, may have annual earnings in the $60,000s.

Since they run their own businesses, owners must pay for their own benefits, such as health insurance and retirement plans.

WORK ENVIRONMENT

Center owners spend a lot of time on their feet, helping staff, directing children, and checking on classrooms. Most child care centers have play areas both inside and outside. In the spring and summer months, owners—especially those with a small staff or none at all—may spend some time outside with the kids, leading them in playground exercises and games. The colder winter months will keep the kids confined mostly indoors. Though child care workers can control the noise somewhat, the work conditions are rarely quiet. An owner's work is divided between child care and administrative responsibilities, but the size of the center often determines how much time is spent on each. For example, the owner of a small service with one part-time employee will spend most of the day with the children, directing activities, serving snacks, settling arguments over toys, and talking with parents as they drop off or pick up their children. For the most part, this owner will do administrative work—record keeping of attendance, billing for services, paying the center's bills, filing tax forms—during short periods of free time in the day and during the evenings and on weekends when the center is closed. Owners of large centers with several staff members often have more time during the day to attend to administrative duties. Even these owners, however, often work on business matters after hours. Nancy Moretti's center is open Monday through Friday, 6:30 A.M. to 6:00 P.M., but she also works weekends. "It's fun most of the time," she says, despite 70- to 80-hour workweeks.

OUTLOOK

The U.S. Department of Labor projects overall employment in the field of child care services to grow much faster than the average for all industries through 2016. More women than ever are part of the workforce; of those who have children, many take only an abbreviated maternity leave. The Children's Defense Fund reports that every day 13 million preschool-aged children in the United States are in some type of child care. By 2010, the nation will have another 1.2 million children aged four and under. Corporations have tried to open their own day care centers for the children of employees but haven't always had much success. Often these corporations turn to outside sources and contract with independent care centers to meet these child care needs.

Staffing problems in general plague the child care industry, as centers struggle to find reliable, long-term employees. Other concerns of child care centers include providing better child care for low-income families; making child care more inclusive for children with disabilities; and possible competition from state-funded prekindergarten programs.

On the bright side, though, licensed child care centers continue to open and provide opportunities for those wanting to run their own businesses. Those centers that offer a number of services, such as after-school programs for older children and computer instruction for children at a variety of age levels, should have the most success and continue to draw new clients.

FOR MORE INFORMATION

For information about the CDA credential, contact
Council for Professional Recognition
2460 16th Street, NW
Washington, DC 20009-3575
Tel: 800-424-4310
http://www.cdacouncil.org

Visit NAEYC's Web site to read relevant articles concerning issues of child care and to learn about membership and accreditation for educational programs.

National Association for the Education of Young Children (NAEYC)
1313 L Street, NW, Suite 500
Washington, DC 20005-4110
Tel: 800-424-2460
http://www.naeyc.org

For information about student memberships and training opportunities, contact

National Association of Child Care Professionals
PO Box 90723
Austin, TX 78709-0723
Tel: 800-537-1118
Email: admin@naccp.org
http://www.naccp.org

For information about the NAC credential and to learn about the issues affecting child care, visit NCCA's Web site or contact

National Child Care Association (NCCA)
2025 M Street, NW, Suite 800
Washington, DC 20036-3309
Tel: 800-543-7161
Email: info@nccanet.org
http://www.nccanet.org

Cleaning Service Owners

QUICK FACTS

School Subjects
Business
Chemistry
Technical/shop

Personal Skills
Leadership/management
Mechanical/manipulative
Technical/scientific

Work Environment
Primarily indoors
Primarily multiple locations

Minimum Education Level
High school diploma

Salary Range
$22,000 to $42,000 to $60,000

Certification or Licensing
Voluntary

Outlook
About as fast as the average

DOT
N/A

GOE
N/A

NOC
N/A

O*NET-SOC
N/A

OVERVIEW

Cleaning service owners go into homes, offices, and apartment buildings to clean carpets, upholstery, and drapes. With special training, they also clean air ducts and restore homes and buildings damaged by fire, flood, and other disasters. There are successful cleaning services all across the country, but those businesses devoted to disaster restoration are generally located in areas with cold seasons and inclement weather.

HISTORY

Before the development of special looms and fibers, carpets and rugs were only for the well-to-do. A rug cleaner had to be very knowledgeable about the weaving and knotting of rugs, and about coloring and dying processes to properly clean and repair rugs. With the invention of "tufting" and synthetic fibers in Georgia in the 1930s, carpet production became more efficient, carpets became cheaper, and sales increased. And carpet cleaning became a service needed in homes and office buildings. Window washing companies were already in business, contracting out to skyscrapers in the big cities, and carpet cleaners followed suit. By the 1960s, companies were offering full-service cleaning—windows, carpets, and drapes. With downsizing in the 1980s, the services of independent cleaning companies replaced many of the custodial crews of large buildings. Better cleaning products have also helped the industry; more powerful machines and cleaning formulas have made work easier and quicker than in the days of waxes and polishes.

THE JOB

Ever try to get a juice stain out of the sofa? Or try lugging a rented rug shampoo machine into your house for a cleaning? Then you have an idea of the demands of a cleaning service. People hire cleaning services to remove dirt and stubborn stains from the carpets in their homes. Cleaners come to your house with their own equipment and chemicals to wash the rugs and vacuum them. They take down drapes, clean them, then rehang them. They restore and refinish hardwood floors. With special high-powered vacuums and brushes, they clean air ducts. In addition to working in homes, they also clean offices and other large public buildings.

To become "The Best Swedish Carpet Cleaner in Phoenix," as his promotions claim, Anders Berg has been building his business for the last 10 years. "It can be feast or famine," he says. "There may be many jobs one day, and none another. But I keep fairly well-booked; I have two to three jobs a day throughout the week." He starts his day at around 7:30 A.M., making phone calls to confirm jobs for the day. In addition to carpet cleaning, Anders offers clients carpet dyeing, upholstery cleaning, duct cleaning, vacuum sales and repair, water and flood restoration, and many other services. He works weekends, holidays, and six-day work weeks. "It's a service business," he says, "so, when you're needed, you respond."

Carpet cleaners use different methods and equipment. For hot water extraction, a hot-water cleaning solution is first sprayed on the carpet. The soil dissolves in the solution, and the solution is then lifted from the carpet with a wet vacuum. Although it's commonly known as "steam" cleaning, no steam is actually generated by the heated solution. Shampooing is another method: It involves applying the cleaning solution to the carpet with a circular brush. The brush spins, rubbing the carpet and frothing the solution into a foam. The soil is then suspended and removed by wet/dry vacuuming. Other methods of carpet cleaning are foam cleaning and dry cleaning.

To clean the carpets of his clients, Berg owns a service truck and a cleaning machine. "Maintaining equipment can be costly," he says. He must also visit a supplier once a week for the chemicals he needs. When dealing with flood and water damage, he uses deodorizers and sanitizers and may have to rent additional equipment for the job.

Some cleaning services specialize in disaster restoration. After a house or building has been damaged by fire, smoke, or flooding, restorers are brought in to clean. With special skills, they work to restore the property to its original state, cleaning and repairing from top to bottom. Walls, ceilings, carpets, and furniture are cleaned. Carpets may be extracted and deodorized. Damaged furniture is reupholstered. Some companies even repair damaged books, documents, electronics, diskettes, and microfilm. Cleaning services that offer restoration often maintain a 24-hour phone number for emergencies.

A cleaning service may contract with a company to clean offices and apartments on a regular basis. They perform the usual cleaning of carpets and drapes and also fire-retard drapes to meet local fire ordinances. They clean fabric walls and fabric partitions. Cleaning services usually only enter office buildings after business hours, so commercial work often involves late evenings and weekends.

"Residential carpet cleaning is nice," Berg says. "You meet different people every day. And most people are appreciative." Anders must regularly promote his services to build up a client base. "I always have to look for new clients," he says, "and try to keep the ones I have. Once upon a time, a CPA would hang out his shingle, and before he knew it, he had clients. It's a more complicated process now. There's more competition." When you're running your own cleaning service, you must also attend to your own administrative concerns, such as scheduling, bookkeeping, and billing. Anders also attends trade fairs in Stockholm and stocks up on new products. He recently brought back a microfiber cloth. The cloth is made of a fine, synthetic material that removes dirt, grease, and oil without chemicals.

REQUIREMENTS

High School

Because the materials, chemicals, and equipment for professional cleaning are likely to become more complicated, you should take courses that will help you adapt to chemical and mechanical advancements. Science courses can teach you about the products you'll be using. You'll be purchasing and using your own equipment, so a vocational class that involves you in mechanics can help you better understand the machines and their repair. Accounting classes and student business organizations will prepare you for the record-keeping aspect of the work. Take English and composition courses to develop writing skills for your own advertising and promotion.

Postsecondary Training

Though this may change in the near future, the cleaning services industry had been typically easy to break into. If you're looking for employment with a cleaning service, you probably won't need any special certification, or even a high school diploma. Even as you develop your own service, you probably won't be hindered by a lack of education or training when seeking clients. As the job becomes more technically demanding, however, training programs will become standard.

Kenway Mead, former executive administrator for the Institute of Inspection, Cleaning and Restoration Certification (IICRC), advises students to get first-hand experience in the business. You should seek out large cleaning businesses that contract their services to companies; these larger companies will be more likely to have good training systems in place. You should look for a company that has some certification and belongs to either regional or national professional organizations. Membership with such an organization will mean the company is privy to training information and requirements.

The IICRC offers seminars and conferences, as does the Restoration Industry Association (RIA). Some technical schools and community colleges offer training for cleaning technicians seeking certification. These schools offer courses in the use and care of cleaning agents, supplies, and equipment, as well as job organization and planning.

Certification or Licensing

Certification isn't required to run a cleaning service, but it can help you attract business. You should either belong to a regional professional association or seek certification with the IICRC or the RIA. Several different categories of certification are available from the IICRC, including carpet cleaning technician, commercial carpet maintenance technician, and upholstery and fabric cleaning technician. The RIA offers the following disaster restoration-related and general certifications: certified mold professional, certified restorer, water loss specialist, certified rug specialist, certified mechanical hygienist, and certified fabric specialist. Because of the special skills required for removing smoke and water from property, restoration certification involves a demanding program of training and testing. Approximately 15 percent of cleaning service workers are certified.

Other Requirements

"I'm an obsessive-compulsive cleaner," Anders Berg says. "That's not my natural language, but I noticed that phrase in someone's profile, and thought it was a really good description. I'm a clean freak." In addition to a love for cleaning, you should also have a talent for it. "In baseball," Berg says, "when a guy doesn't swing [at a ball out of the strike zone], he has a good eye. That's what most people lack in cleaning. People don't vacuum in an organized way. The smarter,

Books to Read

Bewsey, Susan. *Start and Run a Home Cleaning Business.* 2d ed. Bellingham, Wash.: Self-Counsel Press, 2003.

Farmer, Forrest L. *Introduction to Janitorial Service Contracting: How to Succeed in Your Own Cleaning Business.* Portland, Ore.: Clean-Pro Industries Inc., 2000.

Farmer, Forrest L. *Sales and Marketing for Janitorial Service Businesses: Strategies for Promoting, Estimating, and Bidding Cleaning Services.* Portland, Ore.: Clean-Pro Industries Inc., 2000.

Haley, Graham, and Rosemary Haley. *Haley's Cleaning Hints.* New York: Penguin Books, 2004.

Jorstad, Laura, and Melinda Morse. *How to Start a Home-Based Housecleaning Business.* 2nd ed. Guilford, Conn.: Globe Pequot Press, 2005.

Lynn, Jacquelyn. *Start Your Own Cleaning Service.* Newburgh, N.Y.: Entrepreneur Press, 2006.

more efficiently you work, the less time you spend on the task." You also need good business sense and the ability to constantly promote and market your business. You should be friendly with your customers to encourage repeat business.

EXPLORING

There's no shortage of opportunities for you to test your interest in cleaning. Many different organizations in your community need volunteers for such work. The social services department that assists the elderly and the disabled in your town relies on volunteers and part-time workers to go into homes and clean for those who can't do it themselves. Those jobs will generally involve only light cleaning and vacuuming. Because most of your work will involve solutions and equipment, rent a carpet cleaning machine and try it out. Clean all the carpets in your house, and you'll get a sense of the daily duties of a cleaning service owner (though professional cleaning tools are often larger and more complex than the ones you rent from a store). Large cleaning services that clean office buildings and stores often hire high school students for evening hours and weekends. Working even part time, you'll learn a lot about the cleaning equipment and requirements of the work.

EMPLOYERS

Many cleaning services are one-owner operations, but some may hire 40 or more people to assist with corporate contracts or disaster restoration. If you're in business for yourself, you may offer both commercial and residential service, but you're likely to want to choose between the two. If contracted for commercial service (cleaning an office building, a mall, an apartment building, or some other public area), you'll probably sign on for a number of months with a predetermined number of cleanings per week. Working the residential market will involve working with different clients every day.

STARTING OUT

A lot of people who own cleaning services started their own businesses after working in other jobs. With the downsizing of the 1980s, many members of corporate cleaning crews started their own commercial cleaning services after being laid off. Anders Berg has worked in some aspect of the cleaning industry since 1969, mostly in sales and consulting positions. "I had done some carpet cleaning in Sweden," he says. "But it's not as common there. People usually just threw their carpet out." When he moved to Phoenix, a friend suggested he start his own service, which he has now had for more than 25 years.

Start-up costs are relatively low. Depending on the kind of work you'll be doing, the initial expense of your equipment is likely to be much less than $4,000 (not including the van or truck needed for transporting the equipment).

ADVANCEMENT

Once you've established your own business, you'll have to work hard to maintain a customer base and promote your services to expand your clientele. As you gain experience and make connections, you'll be able to expand your business into other areas. Some cleaning services sell cleaning products and vacuums, sell and install new carpet, and offer landscaping and maintenance services. Taking on a number of commercial contracts can mean big money, but it also requires a complete staff. Disaster restoration work for commercial properties can earn millions of dollars for a good, certified restoration service that has the special equipment and a staff of highly skilled technicians.

EARNINGS

Because of the differing sizes of cleaning services, from franchises and one-owner operations, to multimillion dollar cleaning companies, few accurate salary statistics have been compiled. Kenway Mead estimates that a carpet cleaning technician working for a service makes between $8 and $12 per hour, while a hard-working entrepreneur with a single-person operation can make between $42,000 and $60,000 a year. Someone with a disaster restoration service can make a lot more money from contracts with insurance companies, but it's also a lot more work, requiring more staff.

A carpet cleaner providing residential service will charge per room, per hour, or per square foot. Services charge between $20 and $50 per room, with extra charges for disinfectant and fabric protection. To clean upholstery, a cleaner will charge between $30 and $50 for each piece of furniture.

Cleaning service owners must provide their own benefits, such as health and life insurance and a savings and pension program.

WORK ENVIRONMENT

You'll be working with heavy equipment and chemicals that you may be sensitive to. "It's a lot of physical work," Anders Berg says, "and it can be repetitive. You can wear out your legs, your arms, your back." The equipment and vacuums can be noisy. With the exception of hauling your equipment from your truck to the home or building, your work will be primarily inside. If in business for yourself, you won't have any supervision beyond the comments and opinions of your clientele. In most cases, you'll be allowed to work alone in the homes and in unoccupied commercial properties. Most of your work will be routine, but if you also provide disaster restoration, you'll be working in flooded or fire-damaged homes and buildings. With larger projects, you may be working with a team of cleaners and restorers.

Cleaning service owners average 40 hours or more per week. They often work weekends, holidays, and after business hours and occasionally deal with late-night restoration emergencies. When not actually cleaning, owners must devote time to equipment maintenance, record-keeping, and calling clients.

OUTLOOK

The demand for cleaning services has grown steadily over the last 20 years, and this is expected to continue. Office buildings make up the biggest share of the cleaning services market, and the marketplace is expanding to include more government buildings and industrial plants, as well. Cleaning services were listed as one of the best "evergreen businesses" (businesses that are consistently profitable) in a ranking of the top 20 home businesses by *Working at Home Magazine*.

Kenway Mead predicts that the business will become more scientific, requiring a more intensive education. He also anticipates that environmental concerns will mean more business for cleaning services. "Cleaning affects indoor air quality," he points out. The RIA sponsors research into the testing of products, cleaning methods, and toxicity. Less chemical-based cleaning methods are currently in development.

As the science of cleaning advances, more specialization within the market will be required. To best understand your equipment, methods, and solutions, you may need to narrow your services to residential, commercial, or restoration. Restorers who service large businesses will have to keep up with the technology of electronics and information storage in order to best restore office hardware and software.

FOR MORE INFORMATION

For information on certification and cleaning advice, contact
Institute of Inspection, Cleaning and Restoration Certification
2715 East Mill Plain Boulevard
Vancouver, WA 98661-4806
Tel: 360-693-5675
http://www.iicrc.org

For general career information and cleaning facts, visit the RIA's Web site. The RIA also offers certification, conferences, and seminars.
Restoration Industry Association (RIA)
9810 Patuxent Woods Drive, Suite K
Columbia, MD 21046-1595
Tel: 800-272-7012
http://www.ascr.org

Computer Support Service Owners

OVERVIEW

The owners of computer support services help businesses and individuals install and maintain computer hardware and software. They offer advice on what computers to purchase; they teach how to operate computers; and they assist with computer problems as they arise. There are approximately 552,000 computer support specialists in the industry, including technicians and entrepreneurs. *Computer consultants* either work out of their homes, or they rent office space. Though some of their assistance is offered over the phone, much of their work is performed on-site.

HISTORY

Did you know there are museums devoted to "antique" computer hardware? Hang on to those old monitors, keyboards, and hard drives—they may be worth something to collectors and archivists some day. When you think about computers, you are probably not thinking about the past. Computer hardware and software is most often talked about in terms of the future, but computer technology has been in development for more than a century. In 1854, George Boole invented Boolean Algebra, a symbol and logic system used as the basis of computer design.

The 1950s brought IBM's first computers and the computer programming languages COBOL and LISP. By the late 1960s, people with computer skills served as consultants to develop hardware and software for manufacturers. The Independent

48

Computer Consultants Association (ICCA) was founded in 1976. Consultants had many more opportunities when even small businesses began investing in computers. Office software, such as spreadsheet programs and programs that link computers together with a shared hard drive, were developed in the early 1980s. Many businesses and schools required the regular services of computer support technicians by the late 1980s. Today, computer support service workers play an integral role in the success of businesses large and small.

THE JOB

If your computer is not working, the problem may be simply that you have forgotten to plug in the machine. But it can be much more complicated than that, requiring the assistance of someone with a great deal of computer knowledge. Today's hardware and software are easier to use than in previous years, but can be difficult to install correctly and difficult to learn. Computer support service owners use their computer expertise to help businesses and individuals buy new computers and ready them for daily use.

With their operations based in their home office, computer support service owners take calls from new clients, as well as clients who regularly rely on their services. Clients may have problems with their printers not responding to computer commands; a computer may be locked up; they may have problems performing the particular functions their software is designed for. In some cases, support service owners are able to diagnose the problem and offer assistance over the phone. But in most cases, they are required to go to the offices and work hands-on with the computer systems. Armed with a cell phone, pager, and laptop, they drive to the offices of businesses small and large and the homes of personal computer owners to help get the computers running again. They will install network systems and new hardware and software. They upgrade existing systems. Computer support service owners also teach computer operators how to use the new systems, either one on one or in group training sessions. They advise on the purchase of hardware and software, and can prepare backup methods.

Many computer consultants also offer their expertise in Web design and multimedia for uploading a Web page, preparing a presentation, and offering desktop publishing services. They also help to create computer databases. Some computer consultants are involved in issues of programming.

Brad Crotteau started his own computer support service in 1991, and his business has grown into Crocker Networking Solutions Inc.

He anticipated that some of the demands of the job would become more difficult as he got older, so he recently made some decisions about the nature of his business. "I knew I didn't always want to be crawling around, plugging computers in," he says. So Crotteau incorporated his business and took on a staff of nine employees, including technicians, sales people, administrative assistants, trainers, and Web designers.

Crotteau's day starts early at 7:00 A.M. with paperwork, followed at around 8:00 A.M. by phone calls from businesses. He then must work the new requests for service into his daily schedule. Though he has a staff of nine, Crotteau is still actively involved in the technical work of installing systems and troubleshooting, and the generating of estimates and other financial details. He makes it a point to end his workday at 6:00 P.M., though he is required to work some overtime. "I have stayed up until 4:00 A.M.," he says, "bringing a service up for a client, but that's rare." His client base consists of businesses with between five and 85 personal computers. The biggest challenge can be correcting user-generated problems. Crotteau says giving an inexperienced computer user a complex system "is like giving a Maserati to someone who just started riding horses a few weeks ago."

Crotteau's support service is also embarking on a new business venture. He has trademarked many of his company's services, and now offers them as a product called "Performance Net." His company sells the network systems, and then puts the systems into place. This venture has been helped along by a business alliance with a manufacturer of software. Crotteau's company has been hired by the manufacturer to install their servers in businesses all across the country.

In addition to technical work, the owners of computer support services must handle all the details of running their businesses. They handle phone calls, bookkeeping, and client records. They must also research new technologies and keep up-to-date on advanced technical skills. Maintaining connections within the industry is also important; computer support system owners may need to call upon the assistance of other consultants and technicians to help with some projects.

REQUIREMENTS
High School
Of course, you should take any classes that will familiarize you with computers. Computer science classes will help you learn about operating systems and programming. Learn about the various soft-

ware, like word processing and spreadsheet programs, as well as the languages of Web page design. Taking a journalism class and working on your school newspaper will involve you with multimedia presentation and teach you about page layout and graphic design. Take courses in business and accounting to prepare for the book-keeping and administrative details of the work. English composition and communication courses can help you develop teaching skills.

Postsecondary Training

Though a degree is not required for you to start your own computer support service, most service owners and consultants have at least an associate's degree. Some consultants supplement their education with special training offered by computer software companies such as Novell and Microsoft. Many consultants registered with the ICCA have advanced degrees and highly technical training in such areas as robotics, telecommunications, and nuclear engineering. Community colleges and universities across the country have programs in computer science, computer engineering, and electrical engineering. For a degree in computer science, you will be required to take courses in calculus, English composition, program design, algorithms, computer graphics, and database management. Electrical engineering programs include courses in BASIC programming, industrial electronics, digital inte-grated circuits, and microprocessor systems. In addition to seminars, you will also attend labs. Some bachelor's programs include research projects in which you will work closely with a faculty member to study new technologies. Some software companies offer training programs.

Very few consultants start their own businesses straight out of college. Several years working full time as part of a computer service staff will give you the firsthand experience you will need. Not only will you develop your computer expertise, but you will learn what is required to operate a business.

Certification or Licensing

There are many different kinds of certifications available to people working in computer support and consulting. No one certification, however, serves all the varying needs of computer professionals. Some consultants get certified in database design and administra-tion. Some consultants have Microsoft certified system engineer (MCSE) status. Visit http://www.microsoft.com/learning/mcp/mcse for information on the MCSE exam, which tests your understand-ing of Windows networks, hardware requirements and installations, and system maintenance. This certification should only supplement an extensive computer background, not replace it. The term "paper MCSE" has evolved in the industry to describe those who "look good on paper" with their certification, but do not have the networking and computer science education and experience to back it up.

The Institute for Certification of Computer Professionals offers a certified computing professional exam. Nearly 55,000 computer professionals hold the certification, having passed an exam that tests knowledge of business information systems, data resource management, software engineering, and other subjects.

Other Requirements

You should have good business and money management skills. Though some months you may have more work than you can handle, with a steady flow of income, other months there may be no work at all. You will have to budget your money to carry you through the lean months. Though computer skills are very important, you will need good people skills to maintain customer relations.

Teaching skills are important, because you will be training people in how to use their systems. "You need the ability to talk to people in a language they can understand," Brad Crotteau says, "but don't talk down to them. You have to gauge your client's understanding."

EXPLORING

Get to know your own home computer—study the software and its manuals, and familiarize yourself with computer programming languages. Read some of the many magazines devoted to computers, such as *Macworld* (http://www.macworld.com). Find out who services the computers in your school, and ask to spend some time with the technicians. But do not just focus on the technical duties of the people who own computer support services, find out how they go about running an office and maintaining a small business. Join your school's business club and you'll have the opportunity to meet small business owners in your area.

EMPLOYERS

Approximately 552,000 computer support specialists are employed in the United States. Computer support service owners work for a variety of different clients, servicing the personal computers in home-based offices, as well as contracting with large companies for long-term assistance. Though many individuals have computers in their homes for their personal use, few of them seek out professional service. The main clients of support service owners will be accounting firms, insurance agencies, government departments— any business or organization that relies upon computers to perform daily operations. Even a company that has its own full-time support staff will occasionally hire outside consultants. Computer support services are in demand all across the country, but are most successful in large cities, as they can draw from a broader client base.

STARTING OUT

Brad Crotteau had been working for Pacific Gas and Electric as an engineer for 14 years when he began developing his own business on the side. "The main concern for people starting their own businesses," Crotteau says, "is how they're going to capitalize their company." Crotteau was fortunate to receive an early retirement package, and then worked for a while as a computer consultant for a private consulting company. Once he'd felt he'd gotten his feet wet, he was ready to start full time with his own support service. "You should work for a large corporation," Crotteau advises, "to learn about human resources, compensation packages, benefits. You need to develop a good business sense. That's why many small businesses fail. You may be great at computers, but bad at business."

As with many start-ups, it's good for you to focus your talents. Decide on a niche, such as networking, or package customization, then promote those specific services. Crotteau credits much of his success to good marketing techniques, which includes careful attention to image. "You can't do this from the back of your car," he says, "but promoting a good image doesn't have to be expensive. Our biggest sales tool is our business cards. We have a nice, multicolored business card that reads well."

ADVANCEMENT

Once they are established in their niche market, support service owners can expand to include other services. Some computer support services are able to offer much more than technical assistance. They also hold training sessions, prepare multimedia reports and presentations, and design Web pages. The more business connections a support service owner can make with support services, computer manufacturers, and other companies, the better they'll be able to build their client base. As their business grows, support service owners can hire staff to deal with administrative duties, as well as technicians to assist with servicing their clients' computers.

EARNINGS

According to the U.S. Department of Labor, median hourly wages for computer support specialists were $20.39 in 2007, which, based on a 40-hour workweek, is a salary of $42,400 a year. Salaries ranged from less than $25,950 to $69,300 or more annually. Those working in large cities like New York and Los Angeles average more than those in the Midwest, the Southwest, and the Northwest. A computer support specialist in New York with more than 10 years experience can average more than $90,000 a year, while a consultant with similar experience in the Southwest may make closer to $65,000 a year. Some very experienced, business-minded consultants can make $150,000 a year or more.

As self-employed workers, computer support service owners must provide their own benefits, such as health and life insurance and a savings and pension plan.

WORK ENVIRONMENT

Most computer support businesses are based in a home office or a rented commercial space. Computer support service owners devote a lot of time to sitting at their own computer, managing their accounts and records, but the majority of their time will be in the offices of their clients. In either setting, the work environment will likely be quiet and well lit. The work will be indoors, though support service owners will travel from office to office throughout the day.

When installing and repairing computer hardware, support service owners may have to crawl around behind desks to hook up wires and plug in cords. This work is essentially unsupervised, but some clients may ask to receive instruction and information about the repairs being made. In some cases, support service owners may work as part of a team, particularly if they are brought into a large company with a full-time support staff.

Some consultants work much more than 40 hours a week, though support service owners can avoid this by developing strong business management skills. "If you're working 80 hours a week," Brad Crotteau says, "something's wrong. You'll have to work hard, but you don't have to obsess about it."

OUTLOOK

The U.S. Department of Labor predicts that the field of computer support will grow about as fast as the average through 2016. Opportunities should continue to be good as computer systems become more important to many businesses. Lower prices on computer hardware and software will inspire businesses to expand their systems, and to invest in the services needed to keep them up and running. As computer programs become more sophisticated and are able to perform more complex operations, consultants will be needed to help clients operate these programs. With companies relying more on complex computer systems, they will be less likely to take risks in the installation of hardware and software. To stay at the top of the industry, consultants will have to keep up on technological developments and take continuing education courses.

More consultants may also become involved in broadening computer literacy. Computer resources are generally limited to middle-class students; some nonprofit organizations are forming to bring more computers and support services to inner-city youth, low-income families, and people with disabilities.

FOR MORE INFORMATION

To learn more about membership and career training seminars, contact
Association of Computer Support Specialists
333 Mamaroneck Avenue, #129
White Plains, NY 10605-1440
http://www.acss.org

To learn about membership benefits, contact
Independent Computer Consultants Association (ICCA)
11131 South Towne Square, Suite F
St. Louis, MO 63123-7817
Tel: 314-892-1675
Email: execdirector@icca.org
http://www.icca.org

For information on certification programs, contact
Institute for Certification of Computing Professionals
2350 East Devon Avenue, Suite 115
Des Plaines, IL 60018-4610
Tel: 800-843-8227
Email: office@iccp.org
http://www.iccp.org

For resume and cover letter advice, salary statistics, and other career information in information technology, visit
Robert Half Technology
http://www.roberthalftechnology.com

Desktop Publishing Specialists

QUICK FACTS

School Subjects
Art
Computer science
English

Personal Skills
Artistic
Communication/ideas

Work Environment
Primarily indoors
Primarily one location

Minimum Education Level
Some postsecondary training

Salary Range
$20,960 to $35,510 to
$56,950+

Certification or Licensing
None available

Outlook
Little or no change

DOT
979

GOE
01.07.01

NOC
1423

O*NET-SOC
43-9031.00

OVERVIEW

Desktop publishing specialists prepare reports, brochures, books, cards, and other documents for printing. They create computer files of text, graphics, and page layout. They work with files others have created, or they compose original text and graphics for clients. There are approximately 32,000 desktop publishing specialists employed in the United States.

HISTORY

When Johannes Gutenberg invented movable type in the 1440s, it was a major technological advancement. Up until that point, books were produced entirely by monks, every word written by hand on vellum. Though print shops flourished all across Europe with this invention, inspiring the production of millions of books by the 1500s, there was little major change in the technology of printing until the 1800s. By then, cylinder presses were churning out thousands of sheets per hour, and the Linotype machine allowed for easier, more efficient plate-making. Offset lithography (a method of applying ink from a treated surface onto paper) followed and gained popularity after World War II. Phototypesetting, which involved creating film images of text and pictures to be printed, was later developed. At the end of the 20th century, computers caused another revolution in the industry. Laser printers now allow for low-cost, high-quality printing, and desktop publishing software is credited with spurring sales and use of personal home computers.

THE JOB

If you've ever used a computer to design and print a page for your high school paper or yearbook, then you've had some experience in desktop publishing. Not so many years ago, the prepress process (the steps to prepare a document for the printing press) involved metal casts, molten lead, light tables, knives, wax, paste, and a number of different professionals from artists to typesetters. With computer technology, these jobs are becoming more consolidated.

Desktop publishing specialists have artistic talents, proofreading skills, sales and marketing abilities, and a great deal of computer knowledge. They work on computers converting and preparing files for printing presses and other media, such as the Internet and CD-ROM. Much of desktop publishing is called prepress, when specialists typeset, or arrange and transform, text and graphics. They use the latest in design software; programs such as PhotoShop, Illustrator, InDesign (all from software designer Adobe), and QuarkXPress, are the most popular. Some desktop publishing specialists also use CAD (computer-aided design) technology, allowing them to create images and effects with a digitizing pen.

Once they've created a file to be printed, desktop publishing specialists either submit it to a commercial printer or print the pieces themselves. Whereas traditional typesetting costs more than $20 per page, desktop printing can cost less than a penny a page. Individuals hire the services of desktop publishing specialists for creating and printing invitations, advertising and fundraising brochures, newsletters, flyers, and business cards. Commercial printing involves catalogs, brochures, and reports, while business printing encompasses products used by businesses, such as sales receipts and forms.

Typesetting and page layout work entails selecting font types and sizes, arranging column widths, checking for proper spacing between letters, words, and columns, placing graphics and pictures, and more. Desktop publishing specialists choose from the hundreds of typefaces available, taking the purpose and tone of the text into consideration when selecting from fonts with round shapes or long shapes, thick strokes or thin, serifs or sans serifs. Editing is also an important duty of a desktop publishing specialist. Articles must be updated, or in some cases rewritten, before they are arranged on a page. As more people use their own desktop publishing programs to create print-ready files, desktop publishing specialists will have to be even more skillful at designing original work and promoting their professional expertise to remain competitive.

Darryl Gabriel and his wife Maree own a desktop publishing service in Australia. The Internet has allowed them to publicize their business globally. They currently serve customers in their local area and across Australia, and are hoping to expand more into international Internet marketing. The Gabriels use a computer ("But one is not enough," Darryl says), a laser printer, and a scanner to create business cards, pamphlets, labels, books, and personalized greeting cards. Though they must maintain computer skills, they also have a practical understanding of the equipment. "We keep our prices down by being able to re-ink our cartridges," Darryl says. "This takes a little getting used to at first, but once you get a knack for it, it becomes easier."

Desktop publishing specialists deal with technical issues, such as resolution problems, colors that need to be corrected, and software difficulties. A client may come in with a hand-drawn sketch, a printout of a design, or a file on a disk, and he or she may want the piece ready to be posted on the Internet or to be published in a high-quality brochure, newspaper, or magazine. Each format presents different issues, and desktop publishing specialists must be familiar with the processes and solutions for each. They may also provide services such as color scanning, laminating, image manipulation, and poster production.

Customer relations are as important as technical skills. Darryl Gabriel encourages desktop publishing specialists to learn how to use equipment and software to their fullest potential. He also advises them to know their customers. "Try and be as helpful as possible to your customers," he says, "so you can provide them with products that they are happy with and that are going to benefit their businesses." He says it's also very important to follow up, calling customers to make sure they're pleased with the work. "If you're able to relate to what the customers want, and if you encourage them to be involved in the initial design process, then they'll be confident they're going to get quality products."

REQUIREMENTS
High School
Computer classes and design and art classes will help you develop desktop publishing skills. Computer classes should include both hardware and software, since understanding how computers function will help you with troubleshooting and knowing a computer's limits. Through photography classes you can learn about composition, color, and design elements. Typing, drafting, and print shop classes, if available, will also provide you with the opportunity to

gain some indispensable skills. Working on the school newspaper or yearbook will train you on desktop publishing skills as well, including page layout, typesetting, composition, and working under a deadline.

Postsecondary Training

Although a college degree is not a prerequisite, many desktop publishing specialists have at least a bachelor's degree. Areas of study range anywhere from English to graphic design. Some two-year colleges and technical institutes offer programs in desktop publishing or related fields. A growing number of schools offer programs in technical and visual communications, which may include classes in desktop publishing, layout and design, and computer graphics. Four-year colleges also offer courses in technical communications and graphic design. You can enroll in classes related to desktop publishing through extended education programs offered at universities and colleges. These classes, often taught by professionals in the industry, cover basic desktop publishing techniques and advanced lessons on Adobe PhotoShop or QuarkXPress.

Other Requirements

Desktop publishing specialists are detail oriented, possess problem-solving skills, and have a sense of design and artistic skills. "People tell me I have a flair for graphic design and mixing the right color with the right graphics," Darryl Gabriel says.

A good eye and patience are critical, as well as endurance to see projects through to the finish. You should have an aptitude for computers, the ability to type quickly and accurately, and a natural curiosity. In addition, a calm temperament comes in handy when working under pressure and constant deadlines. You should be flexible and be able to handle more than one project at a time.

EXPLORING

Experimenting with your home computer, or a computer at school or the library, will give you a good idea as to whether desktop publishing is for you. Play around with various graphic design and page layout programs. If you subscribe to an Internet service, take advantage of any free Web space available to you and design your own home page. Join computer clubs and volunteer to produce newsletters and flyers for school or community clubs. Volunteering is an excellent way to try new software and techniques as well as gain experience troubleshooting and creating final products. Part-time or summer employment with printing shops and companies that have in-house publishing or printing departments are other great ways to gain experience and make valuable contacts.

EMPLOYERS

Approximately 32,000 desktop publishing specialists are employed in the United States. Desktop publishing specialists work for individuals and small business owners, such as publishing houses, advertising agencies, graphic design agencies, and printing shops. Some large companies also contract with desktop publishing services rather than hire full-time designers. Government agencies such as the U.S. Government Printing Office hire desktop publishing specialists to help produce the large number of documents they publish.

Desktop publishing specialists deal directly with their clients, but in some cases they may subcontract work from printers, designers, and other desktop publishing specialists. They may also work as consultants, working with printing professionals to help solve particular design problems.

Teen Survey on Entrepreneurship

Junior Achievement Worldwide conducts an annual survey of teens regarding entrepreneurship. Here are some of its findings from a recent survey:

- Nearly 67 percent of teens said that they would like to start a business someday.

- Teens realized it could be challenging to start a business—44.1 percent of teens surveyed said that starting a business would be "difficult, but possible."

- More than 81 percent of teens believed that a four-year or graduate degree would help them prepare for a career as an entrepreneur.

- Teens said that they were most motivated to start their own business because they wanted to earn more money or because they did not want to work for someone else.

- Teens cited "hard work and determination" (32 percent) and "business and management skills" (24.4 percent) as the most important skills for successful entrepreneurs.

Source: 2007 Junior Achievement Worldwide Enterprise Poll on Teens and Entrepreneurship

STARTING OUT

To start your own business, you must have a great deal of experience with design and page layout, and a careful understanding of the computer design programs you'll be using. Before striking out on your own, you may want to gain experience as a full-time staff member of a large business. Most desktop publishing specialists enter the field through the production side, or the editorial side of the industry. Those with training as a designer or artist can easily master the finer techniques of production. Printing houses and design agencies are places to check for production artist opportunities. Publishing companies often hire desktop publishing specialists to work in-house or as freelance employees. Working within the industry, you can make connections and build up a clientele.

You can also start out by investing in computer hardware and software, and volunteering your services. By designing logos, letterhead, and restaurant menus, for example, your work will gain quick recognition, and word of your services will spread.

ADVANCEMENT

The growth of Darryl and Maree Gabriel's business requires that they invest in another computer and printer. "We want to expand," Darryl says, "and develop with technology by venturing into Internet marketing and development. We also intend to be a thorn in the side of the larger commercial printing businesses in town."

In addition to taking on more print projects, desktop publishing specialists can expand their business into Web design and page layout for Internet-based magazines.

EARNINGS

There is limited salary information available for desktop publishing specialists, most likely because the job duties of desktop publishing specialists can vary and often overlap with other jobs. The average wage of desktop publishing specialists in the prepress department generally ranges from $15 to $50 an hour. Entry-level desktop publishing specialists with little or no experience generally earn minimum wage. Freelancers can earn from $15 to $100 an hour.

According to the U.S. Department of Labor, median annual earnings of desktop publishing specialists were $35,510 in 2007. The lowest 10 percent earned less than $20,960 and the highest 10 percent earned more than $56,950. Wage rates vary depending on experience, training, region, and size of the company.

Desktop publishing specialists who are self-employed must provide their own benefits, such as health and life insurance and a savings and pension plan.

WORK ENVIRONMENT

Desktop publishing specialists spend most of their time working in front of a computer, whether editing text, or laying out pages. They need to be able to work with other prepress professionals, and deal with clients. Hours may vary depending on project deadlines at hand. Some projects may take just a day to complete, while others may take weeks or months. Projects range from designing a logo for letterhead, to preparing a catalog for the printer, to working on a file for a company's Web site.

OUTLOOK

According to the U.S. Department of Labor, little or no employment change is predicted for desktop publishing specialists through 2016. This is due in part because a growing number of people in all occupations are learning desktop publishing skills and companies (especially smaller membership and trade organizations) are focusing on creating electronic, rather than print, publications.

Desktop publishing specialists will still be needed to satisfy typesetting, page layout, design, and editorial demands. With new equipment, commercial printing shops will be able to shorten the turnaround time on projects and in turn can increase business and accept more jobs. For instance, digital printing presses allow printing shops to print directly to the digital press rather than printing to a piece of film, and then printing from the film to the press. Digital printing presses eliminate an entire step and should appeal to companies who need jobs completed quickly.

QuarkXPress, Adobe InDesign, Macromedia FreeHand, Adobe Illustrator, and Adobe PhotoShop are some programs often used in desktop publishing. Specialists with experience in these and other software will be in demand.

FOR MORE INFORMATION

These organizations are sources of financial support for education and research projects designed to promote careers in graphic communications. For more information, contact

Graphic Arts Education and Research Foundation
1899 Preston White Drive
Reston, VA 20191-5468

Tel: 866-381-9839
Email: gaerf@npes.org
http://www.gaerf.org

Graphic Arts Information Network
200 Deer Run Road
Sewickley, PA 15143-2324
Tel: 800-910-4283
Email: gain@piagatf.org
http://www.gain.net

National Association for Printing Leadership
75 West Century Road, Suite 100
Paramus, NJ 07652-1408
Tel: 800-642-6275
Email: Information@napl.org
http://www.recouncil.org

Society for Technical Communication
901 North Stuart Street, Suite 904
Arlington, VA 22203-1822
Tel: 703-522-4114
Email: stc@stc.org
http://www.stc.org

Visit the following Web site for information on scholarships, competitions, colleges and universities that offer graphic communication programs, and careers:
GRAPHIC COMM CENTRAL
Email: gcc@teched.vt.edu
http://teched.vt.edu/gcc

Florists

QUICK FACTS

School Subjects
Agriculture
Art
Business

Personal Skills
Artistic
Following instructions
Leadership/management

Work Environment
Primarily indoors
Primarily one location

Minimum Education Level
High school diploma

Salary Range
$15,680 to $22,540 to
$34,930+

Certification or Licensing
Recommended (certification)
Required by certain states
(licensing)

Outlook
Decline

DOT
142

GOE
01.04.02

NOC
0621

O*NET-SOC
27-1023.00

OVERVIEW

Florists, or *floral designers*, arrange live or cut flowers, potted plants, foliage, or other decorative items according to basic design principles to make eye-pleasing creations. Designers make such arrangements for birthdays, weddings, funerals, or other occasions. They are employed by local flower shops or larger national chains, grocery stores, or established at-home businesses. Approximately 87,000 floral design workers are employed in the United States.

HISTORY

Flowers have been used for thousands of years as decoration, personal adornment, or for religious purposes. Ancient Egyptians used flowers to honor their many gods and goddesses. Flowers were arranged in low bowls in an orderly, repetitive pattern—flower, bud, foliage, and so on. Special spouted vases were also used to hold flowers. Lotus flowers, also called water lilies, were Egyptian favorites. They came to symbolize sacredness and were associated with Isis, the Egyptian nature goddess. Flowers were sometimes used as decorations for the body, collar, and hair.

Flowers were fashioned into elaborate wreaths and garlands by the ancient Greeks. The best wreathmakers were often commissioned by wealthy Greeks to make wreaths for gifts, awards, or decoration. Chaplets, special wreaths for the head, were especially popular. Cornucopia, a horn-shaped container still used today, were filled with arrangements of flowers, fruits, and vegetables. Flowers arranged into wreaths and garlands were also popular during the Roman period and well through to the Middle Ages.

The Victorian era saw great developments in the art of floral design. There was enormous enthusiasm for flowers, plants, and gardens; the most cultured young ladies were often schooled in the art of flower arrangement. Rules were first established regarding function and design. Magazines and books about floral arrangement were also published during this time. Proper Victorian ladies often had fresh nosegays, or tussie-mussies, a handheld arrangement of tightly knotted flowers, for sentimental reasons, if not to freshen the air. Posy holders, fancy carriers for these small floral arrangements, came into fashion. Some were made of ivory, glass, or mother-of-pearl, and were elaborately decorated with jewels or etchings. Flowers were also made into small arrangements and tucked into a lady's décolletage inside aptly named containers, bosom bottles.

Ikebana, the Japanese art of floral arrangement that was created in the 6th century, has been a principal influence on formal flower arrangement design. Its popularity still continues today. In the 1950s, free-form expression developed, incorporating pieces of driftwood and figurines within arrangements of flowers and live plants.

Floral traditions of the past still have an impact on us today. It is still fashionable to mark special occasions with flowers, be it an anniversary, wedding, or birthday. People continue to use flowers to commemorate the dead. Today's floral arrangements reflect the current style, trends, and tastes. The best floral designers will follow the developing fashions and creatively adapt them to their arrangements.

THE JOB

From simple birthday bouquets to lavish wedding arrangements, floral designers define a sentiment, a mood, or make an impression, using flowers as their medium of expression. Along with live flowers, designers may use silk flowers or foliage, fresh fruit, and twigs or incorporate decorative items such as candles, balloons, ribbons, and stuffed animals to their arrangements. Good equipment—foam, wire, wooden or plastic picks, shears, florist's knife, tape, and a variety of containers—is essential. Techniques such as wiring flower stems or shading the tips of blooms with paint or glitter are often used to give floral arrangements a finished look. Familiarity with different species of flowers and plants, as well as creativity and knowledge of the elements of design are what distinguish a good floral designer.

Floral designers are fortunate to have a number of employment paths from which to choose. Some designers are employed at flower shops, while some opt to work independently. Aurora Gagni, owner of Floral Elegance, is one such entrepreneur. A registered nurse by training but creative by nature, Gagni always enjoyed making crafts. "I would see a picture of a flower arrangement in a magazine and try to duplicate it," she says, "but I would always add and experiment and make it my own creation." Gagni made floral arrangements, wreaths, and displays for family, friends, and coworkers, who in turn would spread word of her abilities. "At one point, I found myself giving bow-making lessons at work!" In time, Gagni had a steady and growing number of customers who relied on her skills.

What persuaded Gagni to give up nursing and go into business for herself? "My kids!" she answers. Indeed, this job perk is an attractive one, especially for someone juggling a career with family. Gagni conducts her business almost entirely from her home, and is available for the "many little things"—driving to and from sports events, delivering forgotten lunch boxes, and, of course, homework.

Gagni tackles a variety of floral requests, but weddings are her specialty. While a typical wedding day lasts a few hours, the planning stage can take months. "Usually, the bride and groom look at my book," Gagni says, "and decide if they like my work." If so, the contract is "closed"—the contract agreement is signed, a budget is set, and a down payment is made—several months before the wedding day. Soon after, designs are made, keeping the budget in mind. Many brides wish for orchids with a carnation budget. "I try to accommodate what type of flower, or color, or look the customer wants," Gagni explains, "sometimes making alternate suggestions, especially if price is an issue, or if the flower is difficult to obtain." Gagni orders necessary supplies weeks in advance and scouts for upcoming sales. She notifies her floral wholesalers in advance of any flowers that are seasonal or difficult to obtain. Also, she visits the church and reception hall to check on details such as size, location, and any restrictions. The quickest route to both destinations is also mapped out to ensure prompt delivery of the flowers.

Gagni periodically checks in with the bride about any last-minute changes. Oftentimes, more corsages or more banquet table centerpieces are needed to accommodate extra guests. Bows are tied and secured with wire about two weeks before the wedding. Three days before the wedding, flowers are picked and kept fresh in buckets of water treated with floral preservatives. The actual arranging, done in Gagni's basement, is begun the night before the wedding—bricks of floral foam, treated with water and preservatives, keep the flowers in place. Bouquets and corsages are delivered to the bride's home

Industry Segments, 2006

Type of Business	Number of Establishments
Retail Florist Shops	22,753
Supermarkets	21,783
Plant Nurseries/Garden Centers	16,432
Domestic Floriculture Growers	10,563
Floral Wholesalers	900

Source: Society of American Florists

on the morning of the wedding; and ribbons, flower arrangements, and corsages for the groom's party, are brought to the location of the ceremony. Gagni then goes to the hall to set up for the reception. Final touch-ups are given to table centerpieces, the head table is decorated, and the last details are tackled.

Gagni hires additional help for large contracts, especially to assist with the final arrangements. Her children also help when needed, and her husband is her unofficial delivery driver.

Most retail floral businesses keep a relatively small staff. Sales workers help customers place their orders; they also take care of phone orders. Drivers are hired to make deliveries. Sometimes assistant designers are employed.

REQUIREMENTS

High School
Take art and design classes while in high school. After all, "creativity" is an important buzzword in this industry. Biology classes would be helpful in learning about plants and flowers. Do you have aspirations of owning a flower establishment? Sign up for business-related courses and computer classes—they will help make you a better entrepreneur.

Postsecondary Training
In the past, floral designers learned their craft on the job, usually working as an assistant or apprentice to an experienced designer. Most designers today, however, pursue advanced education resulting in a certificate or degree. While this education is not mandatory in the industry, it does give candidates an advantage when they apply for design positions. There are numerous universities that offer degrees

in floriculture and horticulture, as well as community colleges and independent schools that offer certification in floral design.

Programs vary from school to school, lasting anywhere from days to years depending on the type of degree or certificate. For example, the American Floral Art School (http://www.americanfloralartschool.com), a state-approved and licensed vocational school in Chicago, offers courses in modern floral design, with class schedules from one to three weeks. The curriculum includes the fundamentals of artistic floral design, general instruction in picking or wiring, tinting, and arranging flowers, different types of arrangements and their containers, fashion flowers and wedding flowers, and flower shop management. When you are choosing a school to attend, consider the course offerings as well as your career goals. For example, the Boston-based Rittners School of Floral Design (http://www .floralschool.com) offers classes that emphasize floral business skills, a must if you plan on starting your own shop. Some distance education is also available. The Society of American Florists has an online learning center through which various courses are offered.

Certification or Licensing
The American Institute of Floral Designers (AIFD) offers the accredited in floral design designation to applicants who complete an open-book test and participate in evaluation sessions in which they create designs in the following categories: Sympathy Design, Arrangement, Wedding, Flowers to Wear, and Designer's Choice. Contact the AIFD for more information.

Owners of floral shops in some states may need to apply for a business license. Individual states or communities may have zoning codes or other regulations specifying what type of business can be located in a particular area. Check with your state's chamber of commerce or department of revenue for more information on obtaining a license, or visit this Web site: http://www.sba.gov/hotlist/license.html.

Other Requirements
Most people don't wake up one morning and decide to become a floral designer. If you don't have creative and artistic inclinations, you're already a step behind the rest. A good floral designer enjoys and understands plants and flowers, and can visualize a creation from the very first daffodil. Are you able to work well under pressure and deadlines, and effectively deal with vendors or wholesalers? These are daily requirements of the job. Also, be prepared to greet and accommodate all types of customers, from impatient grooms to nervous brides to grieving families. A compassionate and patient personality will help you go far in this field.

A florist unwraps fresh flowers for arrangements he is preparing for Valentine's Day. *(Phelan M. Ebenhack, AP Photo)*

EXPLORING

Considering a future in floral design? Now is the best time to determine if this career is the right one for you. As a high school student without experience, it's doubtful you'll be hired as a floral designer; but working as a cashier, flower delivery person, or an assistant is a great way to break into the industry.

What about taking some classes to test your talent? Michaels, a national arts and crafts retailer, offers floral design workshops. Look for similar workshops in your area. Park district programs also have design classes, especially during the holiday seasons. Such programs are relatively inexpensive—most times the fee is just enough to cover materials used in class.

Learn the industry firsthand—why not spend a day at work with a floral designer? Explain your interest to your local florist and ask if he or she would be willing to let you observe.

EMPLOYERS

Approximately 87,000 floral designers are employed in the United States. Small, independently owned flower shops are the most common employers of florists. Large, national chains, such as Teleflora and FTD, supply additional jobs. Flower departments, now a staple

Where Do Fresh Flowers Come From?

Seventy-nine percent of fresh flowers in the United States come from foreign countries. The top exporters of flowers to the United States are:

- Columbia: 59 percent
- Ecuador: 18 percent
- Netherlands: 9 percent
- Costa Rica: 3 percent
- Canada: 3 percent
- Mexico: 3 percent

The majority (73 percent) of fresh flowers that are grown in the United States come from California. Other popular states include Washington (5 percent), Florida (5 percent), Hawaii (4 percent), Oregon (3 percent), and New Jersey (2 percent).

Source: Society of American Florists

in larger grocery stores, also employ floral designers. Approximately 33 percent of floral designers are self-employed.

STARTING OUT

Some floral designers get their start by working as assistant designers. Others, especially if they are certified, may be hired as floral designers. Experienced designers may concentrate in a certain area, such as weddings, and become wedding specialists.

Aurora Gagni needed to apply for a tax identification number before she officially "opened" her business. This number is necessary to establish accounts with wholesalers and greenhouses, as well as for tax purposes. It would be wise to consult with business or legal experts regarding income tax issues, promotion and advertising, and other matters dealing with operating your own business.

Professionals in floral design maintain a portfolio of their best designs. A portfolio is useful when applying for membership in floral associations, classes, and when wooing potential clients.

ADVANCEMENT

Advancement in this field depends on the interest of the individual. Some floral designers are content to work at small local shops, especially if they have created a name for themselves in the area they serve. Others decide to try employment with larger national chains such as Teleflora, or 1-800-FLOWERS. Superstore grocery chains now boast full-service floral departments, creating many job opportunities for designers.

Do you possess an entrepreneurial nature? Maybe owning a floral business—either based in your home or established in the middle of your town's business district—is in your future. Still other options include entering the field of landscape design; interior landscaping for offices, shopping centers, and hotels; or a large floral design specialty. Imagine working on a float for Pasadena's Tournament of Roses Parade.

Many of Aurora Gagni's contracts are for weddings, so it makes sense that her business branches out accordingly. Party favors, cake toppers, and the veil and cord—elements unique in many ethnic wedding ceremonies—are some items Gagni customizes for her clients.

EARNINGS

Experience counts for a lot when it comes to a designer's salary. Geographic location also plays a part in salary differences. Floral designers on the East and West Coasts traditionally enjoy higher than average salaries, compared to floral designers in other parts of the United States. Stores located in large urban areas tend to have higher annual sales than those in rural areas, resulting in higher pay for their employees.

According to the U.S. Department of Labor, florists had median annual earnings of $22,540 in 2007. Well-established floral designers with a steady customer base can earn more than $34,930 annually. Less experienced florists may earn less than $15,680 annually. The department also reports that florists employed in grocery stores earned a mean annual salary of $25,890 in 2007. Depending on the store, designers may be offered sick leave and vacation time, health and life insurance, as well as other benefits.

WORK ENVIRONMENT

Flowers can be purchased almost anywhere, from small strip-mall flower shops to large national chains to the neighborhood grocery store. This availability means that floral designers can work almost anywhere—from remote, rural areas to busy cities.

Retail floral designers can expect to have comfortable work surroundings. Most floral shops are cool, clean, and well decorated to help attract customers. Glass refrigerators filled with fresh flowers, live plants and flower arrangements, and arts and crafts are typical items in any flower shop. Work stations for making floral pieces are usually found in the back of the store, along with supplies, containers, and necessary equipment.

Expect to spend the majority of the time on your feet—either standing while working on an arrangement, consulting with customers regarding types of flowers, or on a flower-buying expedition. Most retail-based designers work a normal eight-hour workday with a day off during the week. Weekends are especially busy (often because of weddings) and holidays notoriously so. Christmas, Mother's Day, and Valentine's Day are peak times for floral orders. Long work hours are the norm during these times to accommodate the heavy demand for flowers.

Most designers, if contracted to work a wedding, will travel to the church or the banquet hall to make sure the church arrangements or the table arrangements are properly set up.

OUTLOOK

Employment in floral design is expected to decline through 2016, according to the U.S. Department of Labor. Despite this prediction, there should continue to be good opportunities as many florists leave the field for design positions that offer higher pay and more opportunities for advancement (advancement in this career is limited for florists who do not pursue management positions or open their own business). The emergence of full-service floral departments in grocery stores, as well as opportunities in Internet floral shops, have also contributed to job availability. Floral experts who are able to create exciting and original designs will be in high demand. Certified designers may have an edge for the best jobs.

A growing population with large disposable incomes is good news for this industry. Sending flowers to mark an occasion is an old tradition that still has impact today. The increase in lavish weddings and other events, as well as the growing demand for high-quality artificial flower decorations in homes and businesses, will create new jobs for florists.

FOR MORE INFORMATION

For information on accreditation, student chapters, and scholarships available through the AIFD Foundation, contact
American Institute of Floral Designers (AIFD)
720 Light Street
Baltimore, MD 21230-3850
Tel: 410-752-3318

Email: AIFD@assnhqtrs.com
http://www.aifd.org

For education information, including online courses offered through the SAF, contact
Society of American Florists (SAF)
1601 Duke Street
Alexandria, VA 22314-3406
Tel: 703-836-8700
Email: info@safnow.org
http://www.safnow.org

For fun and interesting information about flowers, visit the SAF's Aboutflowers.com Web site.
Aboutflowers.com
http://www.aboutflowers.com

INTERVIEW

Tom Simmons, AIFD, is the former president of the American Institute of Floral Designers. He discussed his career with the editors of Careers in Focus: Entrepreneurs.

Q. Tell us about yourself and your professional background.

A. I have been in the floral industry for more than 25 years. I now own a special event company that specializes in weddings, parties, corporate functions, and educational seminars. I am also an educational specialist for Teleflora, a Flowers by Wire business, traveling across North America, giving seminars geared toward retail florists about all facets of the floral industry. My floral designs have been published in numerous floral magazines and other design magazines in the United States and Canada. Basically self-taught, I did take a few select design courses to fine-tune my skills.

Q. How/where did you get your first job in this field? What did you do?

A. I was a freshman in college looking for a part-time job, so I went to the job bulletin board in the school cafeteria and saw a posting for a local flower shop in need of a part-time floral delivery driver. The ad stated there would be flexible hours and days. The flower shop was a full-service business (weddings, get well flowers, birthdays, and sympathy flowers) and was very close to campus as well as on my way home.

Q. **Can you describe a typical day in your work life as a floral designer?**

A. As a special event floral designer, my day starts with scheduling appointments for potential clients as well as follow-up of confirmed clients for events. During these consultations, I use a great number of photographs of previous events, as well as magazines and reference books with photos, to guide and assist in the selling process to the client. Then there are phone calls and emails to floral wholesale houses to place an order for flowers and foliages that would be used for an event. I also have to purchase containers, vases, and other supplies to create the floral arrangements; organize labor to produce and install the events that are scheduled for the week; and communicate with the event site such as a hotel, church, country club, or private residence. All floral designs are checked for proper water levels and placed, if necessary, in refrigeration.

Q. **What are the most important personal and professional qualities for people in your career?**

A. People in this field should be courteous, polite, and willing to go that extra step with service. You should be knowledgeable about the products that you sell, know the correct names and availability of products and correct prices for all materials, be able to give good care and handling procedures and instructions for all products you sell (cut flowers and plants), and give the best value for the customer's dollar.

Q. **What activities would you suggest to high school students who are interested in this career?**

A. Approach a retail flower shop and volunteer for after school or weekends. Attend local garden club presentations or greenhouse and garden center demonstrations regarding plants. Previous employment in a gift shop or similar retail store can also be beneficial for dealing with customers face to face.

Q. **What is the future employment outlook for floral designers? How is the field changing?**

A. With the constant changing of retail in general and the growth of mass merchandisers (Wal-Mart, Costco), product availability is everywhere and the consumers have more choices. The World Wide Web has also allowed consumers to be a little more experienced about flowers and how to purchase flowers. Mass merchandisers offer employees competitive salaries and benefits. They also expose employees to more corporate environment than a traditional retail flower shop.

As far as the employment outlook, getting the correct education from respectable colleges, universities, or other floral design schools and taking design classes, as well as classes dealing with marketing and business, prepares students for the changing industry. Creating a specialty in the retail florist is what sets creative floral designers apart. The niche market part of the industry is selecting a part (i.e., special events, corporate business, sympathy flower business) that interests the individual. Those specific areas of the industry are the focus for the future.

Franchise Owners

School Subjects
Business
Mathematics

Personal Skills
Following instructions
Leadership/management

Work Environment
Primarily indoors
Primarily one location

Minimum Education Level
Some postsecondary training

Salary Range
$0 to $30,000 to $100,000+

Certification or Licensing
Required by certain
franchisers (certification)
Required by certain states
(licensing)

Outlook
About as fast as the average

DOT
N/A

GOE
N/A

NOC
N/A

O*NET-SOC
N/A

OVERVIEW

A *franchise owner* contracts with a company to sell that company's products or services. After paying an initial fee and agreeing to pay the company a certain percentage of revenue, the franchise owner can use the company's name, logo, and guidance. McDonald's, Subway, and KFC are some of the top franchised companies that have locations all across the country. Franchises, however, are not limited to the fast food industry. Today, franchises are available in a wide variety of business areas including computer service, lawn care, real estate, and even hair salons. According to a survey by PricewaterhouseCoopers, the franchising sector creates 18 million jobs in the United States and yields $1.53 trillion in economic output annually.

HISTORY

Know anybody with an antique Singer sewing machine? Chances are, it was originally sold by one of the first franchise operations. During the Civil War, the Singer Sewing Machine Company recognized the cost-efficiency of franchising and allowed dealers across the country to sell its sewing machines. Coca-Cola, as well as the Ford Motor Company and other automobile manufacturers, followed Singer's lead in the early 20th century by granting individuals the rights to sell their products. Franchising, however, didn't fully catch on until after World War II, when the needs for products and services across the country boomed, right along with the population. Ray Kroc jumped on the bandwagon with his McDonald's restaurants in the 1950s. Since then, the McDonald's franchise has become one of the top moneymaking franchise opportunities of all time.

Franchises have changed somewhat over the last 20 to 30 years. Abuses of the franchise system brought new government regulations in the 1970s, and the government has been actively involved in protecting the rights of both franchisers and franchisees. Also, single-unit ownership, the "mom and pop" operations, is giving way to multiple-unit ownership; a majority of franchisees now own more than one of the franchiser's units.

THE JOB

Today, industry experts report that franchises are responsible for nearly 50 percent of all retail sales in the United States, and this figure is expected to grow through the 21st century. *Franchisers* (those companies that sell franchise businesses) and *franchisees* (those who buy the businesses) are sharing in the more than $1.5 trillion a year that franchise businesses take in. While everyone probably has a favorite business or two—maybe the neighborhood Krispy Kreme with its fresh crullers or the 7-11 down the street with its gallon-sized sodas—not everyone may realize that these are franchised establishments. For those interested in starting their own businesses, becoming franchisees may offer just the right mix of risk and security. Any new business venture comes with a certain amount of risk, but franchises offer the new owners the security of a name and product that customers are used to and are willing to seek out. Someone with money to invest, the willingness to work hard and sometimes long hours, and the desire to operate a retail business may be able to become the successful franchisee, sharing in the franchiser's success.

There's a franchise for practically every type of product and service imaginable. In addition to the familiar McDonald's and Burger King, other franchise operations exist: businesses that offer temporary employment services, maid services, weight control centers, and custom picture framing, to name a few. The International Franchise Association (IFA), in fact, reports that there are approximately 75 different industries that make use of the franchise system. No matter what business a person is interested in, there are probably franchise opportunities available.

Depending on the size and nature of the franchise, owners' responsibilities will differ. Those who are able to make a large initial investment may also be able to hire managers and staff members to assist them. Those running a smaller business will need to handle most, if not all, of the job responsibilities themselves. Though there should be assistance from the franchiser in terms of training, marketing guidance, and established business systems, the business is essentially the franchisee's own. The franchisee has paid an initial franchise fee, makes royalty payments to the franchiser, purchased equipment, and rented business space. Any franchisee must handle administrative details, such as record-keeping, creating budgets, and preparing reports for the franchiser. A franchisee is also responsible for hiring (and firing) employees, scheduling work hours, preparing payroll, and keeping track of inventory. Using the franchiser's marketing methods, the franchisee advertises the business. The practices and systems of franchisers differ, so those interested in this work need to carefully research the franchise before buying into it.

Some owners work directly with the clientele. Of course, someone who owns multiple units of the McDonald's franchise probably won't be taking orders at the counter; but someone who owns a single unit of a smaller operation, like a pool maintenance service, may be actively involved in the work at hand, in dealing with the customers, and in finding new customers.

Donna Weber of Redmond, Washington, owns a Jazzercise franchise. Jazzercise is the world's largest dance fitness franchise corporation, with 6,800 instructors leading more than 30,000 classes weekly in 30 countries. "I own and teach seven Jazzercise classes a week in two suburbs around the Seattle area," Weber says. After investing with an initial low franchise fee, Weber went through considerable training and testing; the training involves instruction on exercise physiology, dance/exercise technique, and safety issues, as well as instruction on the business aspect of owning a franchise. After training, Weber received certification and started her business. She pays a monthly fee to Jazzercise and in return receives choreography notes to new songs and videos demonstrating the exercises.

In addition to conducting classes, Weber spends some part of every workday preparing paperwork for the corporate headquarters. "I keep track of my students' attendance and write personal postcards to those I haven't seen in a while, those who are having birthdays, those who need some personal recognition for a job well done, etc.," says Weber, who must also regularly learn new routines. "I teach three different formats," she says, "regular aerobics, step, and a circuit-training class each week, so there is a lot of prep to do a good, safe class."

The franchisee's experience will be affected by the name recognition of the business. If it's a fairly new business, the franchisee may have to take on much of the responsibility of promoting it. If it is a well-established business, customers and clients already know what to expect from the operation.

REQUIREMENTS

High School

Business, math, economics, and accounting courses will be the most valuable to you in preparing for franchise ownership. Before buying into a franchise, you'll have to do a lot of research into the company, analyzing local demographics to determine whether a business is a sound investment. English classes will help you develop the research skills you'll need. In addition, you will need to hone your communication skills, which will be essential in establishing relationships with franchisers and customers. Take computer classes since it is virtually impossible to work in today's business world without knowing how to use a computer or the Web. If you already know of a particular area that interests you—such as food service, fashion, or, like Donna Weber, fitness—take classes that will help you learn more about it. Such classes may include home economics, art, dance, or physical education.

Postsecondary Training

Because there is such a variety of franchise opportunities available, there is no single educational path for everyone to take on the road to owning a franchise. Keep in mind, however, that when franchisers review your application for the right to purchase a unit, they'll take into consideration your previous experience in the area. Obviously, a real estate company is unlikely to take a risk on you if you've never had any experience as a broker. In addition, there are some franchise opportunities that require degrees; for example, to own an environmental consulting agency, a business which helps companies meet government environmental standards, you'll have to be an engineer or geologist (careers that, in most cases, require at least a bachelor's degree). But there are also many companies willing to sell to someone wanting to break into a new business. Franchisers will often include special training as part of the initial franchise fee.

Experts in the field stress the importance of gaining work experience before starting out with your own business. Hone your sales, management, and people skills and take the time to learn about the industry that interests you. Even if you don't plan on getting a college degree, consider taking some college-level courses in subjects such as business and finance. One recent survey of franchisees found that more than 80 percent had attended college or had a college degree. This reflects the fact that many franchisees have worked for many years in other professions to have the money and security needed for starting new businesses. Some organizations and schools, for example, the Schulze School of Entrepreneurship at the University of St. Thomas (http://www.stthomas.edu/business/schulzeschool/default.html), offer courses for prospective franchisees.

Certification or Licensing

Some franchisers have their own certification process and require their franchisees to go through training. You may also want to receive the certification certified franchise executive offered by the Institute for Certified Franchise Executives, an organization affiliated with the IFA. This certification involves completing a certain number of courses in topics such as economics and franchise law, participating in events such as seminars or conventions, and work experience. Although certification is voluntary, it will show your level of education and commitment to the field as well as give you the opportunity to network with other franchise professionals.

You may also need to obtain a small business license to own a franchise unit in your state. Regulations vary depending on the state and the type of business, so it is important that you check with your state's licensing board for specifics before you invest in a franchise.

Other Requirements

As with any small business, you need self-motivation and discipline to make your franchise unit successful. Though you'll have some help from your franchiser, the responsibilities of ownership are your own. You'll also need a good credit rating to be eligible for a bank loan, or you'll need enough money of your own for the initial investment. You should be fairly cautious—many people are taken every year in fraudulent franchise schemes. But at the same time, you should feel comfortable taking some risks.

EXPLORING

One relatively easy way to learn about franchising is to do some research on the Web. The International Franchise Association, for example, hosts a very informative Web site (http://www.franchise.org). The association also offers the magazine *Franchising World*. Also, check out your public library or bookstores for the many business magazines that report on small business opportunities. Many of these magazines, such as *Entrepreneur* (http://www.entrepreneur.com), publish special editions dealing specifically with franchises.

Join your high school's business club, a group that may give you the opportunity to meet business leaders in your community. Find a local franchise owner and ask to meet with him or her for an information interview. Discuss the pros and cons of franchise ownership, find out about the owner's educational and professional

Books to Read

Blanchard, Ken, Don Hutson, and Ethan Willis. *The One Minute Entrepreneur: The Secret to Creating and Sustaining a Successful Business.* New York: Doubleday Business, 2008.

Canfield, Jack, Mark Victor Hansen, Dahlynn McKowen, and Tom Hill. *Chicken Soup for the Entrepreneur's Soul: Advice and Inspiration on Fulfilling Dreams.* Santa Barbara, Calif.: Chicken Soup for the Soul, 2006.

Jones, Katina Z. *The 200 Best Home Businesses: Easy To Start, Fun To Run, Highly Profitable.* 2nd ed. Cincinnati, Ohio: Adams Media Corporation, 2005.

Lesonsky, Rieva. *Start Your Own Business.* 4th ed. Newburgh, N.Y.: Entrepreneur Press, 2007.

Stephenson, James. *202 Services You Can Sell for Big Profits.* Newburgh, N.Y.: Entrepreneur Press, 2005.

Stephenson, James. *Ultimate Homebased Business Handbook: How to Start, Run and Grow Your Own Profitable Business.* Newburgh, N.Y.: Entrepreneur Press, 2004.

Stephenson, James. *Ultimate Start-Up Directory.* 2nd ed. Newburgh, N.Y.: Entrepreneur Press, 2007.

Weltman, Barbara. *The Complete Idiot's Guide to Starting a Home-Based Business.* 3rd ed. New York: Alpha, 2007.

background, and ask them for general advice. Also, most franchise companies will send you brochures about their franchise opportunities. Request some information and read about what's involved in owning a franchise unit.

Think about what industry interests you, such as services, fast food, health and fitness, or computers. Come up with your own ideas for a franchise business and do some research to find out if this business already exists. If it does, there may be a part-time or summer job opportunity there for you. If it doesn't, keep the idea in mind for your future but go ahead and get some work experience now. Many franchises hire high school students, and even if you end up working at a Subway when what you're really interested in is lawn care, you'll still be gaining valuable experience dealing with customers, handling sales, and working with others.

EMPLOYERS

There are a number of franchise directories available that list hundreds of franchise opportunities in diverse areas. While some franchisers sell

The owner of Curves, a no-frills fitness club for women, stands in her shop. *(Pat Wellenbach, AP Photo)*

units all across the country, others only do business in a few states. Some of the most successful franchises can guarantee a franchisee great revenue, but these franchise units can require hundreds of thousands of dollars in initial investment.

Many franchisees own more than one franchise unit with a company; some even tie two different franchises together in a practice called "cross-branding." For example, a franchisee may own a pizza franchise, as well as an ice cream franchise housed in the same restaurant. Another combination owners find popular is having a convenience store that also houses a fast food outlet.

STARTING OUT

Before you invest a cent, or sign any papers, you should do extensive research into the franchise, particularly if it's a fairly new company. There are many disreputable franchise operations, so you need to be certain of what you're investing in. Lawyers and franchise consultants offer their services to assist people in choosing franchises; some consultants also conduct seminars. The Federal Trade Commission publishes *A Consumer Guide to Buying a Franchise* and other relevant publications. The IFA also provides free franchise-buying advice.

You'll need money for the initial franchise fee and for the expenses of the first few years of business. You may pursue a loan from a bank, from business associates, or you may use your own savings. In some cases your start-up costs will be very low; in others you'll need money for a computer, rental of work space, equipment, signs, and staff. According to the IFA, total start-up costs can range from $20,000 or less to more than $1,000,000, depending on the franchise selected and whether it is necessary to own or lease real estate to operate the business. Moreover, the initial franchise fee for most franchisers is between $20,000 and $28,000.

Some franchises can cost much less. Donna Weber's Jazzercise franchise required an initial $600 franchise fee. Though her business has been successful, she must share her gross income. "Twenty percent of that goes back to Jazzercise each month as a fee, I pay about 23 percent of the gross for monthly rent, and 8.6 percent to the state of Washington for sales tax collected on the price of my tickets. There are lots of women grossing $75,000 a year doing this, and there are some who choose to do this for fun and make nothing in return. It's all in how you make it work for you."

ADVANCEMENT

A new franchise unit usually takes a few years to turn profitable. Once the business has proven a success, franchisees may choose to invest in other franchise units with the same company. Franchise owners may also be able to afford to hire management and other staff to take on some of the many responsibilities of the business.

EARNINGS

The earnings for franchisees vary greatly depending on such factors as the type of franchise they own, the amount of money a franchisee was able to initially invest without taking a loan, the franchise's location, and the number of franchise units the franchisee owns. An International Franchise Association survey of 1,000 franchise owners found that the average yearly salary of this group was $91,630. Approximately 24 percent made more than $100,000 annually.

Since franchisees run their own businesses, they generally do not have paid sick days or holidays. In addition, they are typically responsible for providing their own insurance and retirement plans.

WORK ENVIRONMENT

Owning a franchise unit can be demanding, requiring work of 60 to 70 hours a week, but owners have the satisfaction of knowing that their business's success is a result of their own hard work. Some people look for franchise opportunities that are less demanding and may only require a part-time commitment. "I'm not getting rich," Donna Weber says, "but I love my job, and I love being my own boss. I can schedule my vacations when I want; we usually don't close our classes down, so we hire certified Jazzercise substitutes."

Franchise owners who handle all the business details personally may consider this work to be very stressful. In addition, dealing with the hiring, management, and sometimes firing of staff can also be difficult. In some situations, much of a franchisee's work will be limited to an office setting; in other situations, such as with a home inspection service or a maid service, the franchisee drives to remote sites to work with clients. Some franchises are mobile in nature, and these will involve a lot of traveling within a designated region.

OUTLOOK

While some experts say that the success rate of franchises is very high and a great deal of money can be made with a franchise unit, others say franchising isn't as successful as starting an independent business. According to the U.S. Department of Commerce, less than 5 percent of franchised outlets have failed each year since 1971. However, when reporting figures, franchisers don't always consider a unit as failing if it is under different ownership, but still in operation. The employment outlook will depend on factors such as the economy—a downturn in the economy is always most difficult for new businesses—as well as the type of franchise. Overall, though, growth should be steady and about as fast as the average.

FOR MORE INFORMATION

For information about buying a franchise and a list of AAFD-accredited franchisers, contact
American Association of Franchisees & Dealers (AAFD)
PO Box 81887
San Diego, CA 92138-1887
Tel: 800-733-9858
Email: Benefits@aafd.org
http://www.aafd.org

Visit the FTC's Web site for information on franchising, including the publication A Consumer Guide to Buying a Franchise.
Federal Trade Commission (FTC)
600 Pennsylvania Avenue, NW
Washington, DC 20580-0001

Tel: 877-382-4357
http://www.ftc.gov

*For more information on franchising as well as a free newsletter,
contact*
FranchiseHelp
101 Executive Boulevard, 2nd Floor
Elmsford, NY 10523-1302
Tel: 800-401-1446
Email: company@franchisehelp.com
http://www.franchisehelp.com

For information on certification, contact
Institute for Certified Franchise Executives
1501 K Street, NW, Suite 350
Washington, DC 20005-1412
http://www.franchise.org/certification.aspx

*For general information about franchising, specific franchise oppor-
tunities, and publications, contact the IFA.*
International Franchise Association (IFA)
1501 K Street, NW, Suite 350
Washington, DC 20005-1412
Tel: 202-628-8000
Email: ifa@franchise.org
http://www.franchise.org

To learn about membership for women entrepreneurs, contact
National Association of Women Business Owners
8760 Old Meadow Road, Suite #500
McLean, VA 22102-5120
Tel: 800-55-NAWBO
Email: national@nawbo.org
http://www.nawbo.org

*SIFE is an "international organization that mobilizes university stu-
dents around the world to make a difference in their communities
while developing the skills to become socially responsible business
leaders." Visit its Web site for more information.*
Students in Free Enterprise (SIFE)
http://www.sife.org

Greeting Card Designers and Writers

OVERVIEW

Greeting card designers and writers either work as freelancers or as staff members of greeting card and gift manufacturers. Designers use artistic skills to create illustrated or photographic images for cards, posters, mugs, and other items generally sold in card shops; writers compose the expressions, poems, and jokes that accompany the images. The Greeting Card Association estimates that there are approximately 3,000 large and small greeting card publishers in America.

HISTORY

The Valentine is considered by many to be the earliest form of greeting card. Up until the 5th century, Romans celebrated a fertility festival called Lupercalia every February 15. At the feast, women wrote love notes and dropped them in an urn; the men would pick a note from the urn, then seek the company of the woman who composed the note. But the mass-produced holiday cards we know today didn't originate until the 1880s in England and America. With printing costs and postage rates low, the colorful, cheerful, and beautifully illustrated cards of the day quickly grew in popularity.

THE JOB

From sincere statements of love to jocular jabs, the contemporary greeting card industry provides a note for practically every expression. Hallmark and American Greetings are the biggest names in the business, offering traditional cards and electronic cards (known as e-cards) for many occasions. Other card companies have carved out their own individual niches, like C-Ya, which sells "relationship closure cards" to send to ex-boyfriends and ex-girlfriends, former bosses, and anybody you don't ever want to see again. Though some of these companies use the talents of full-time staff writers and designers, others rely on freelancers to submit ideas, images, and expressions. In addition to greeting card production, some companies buy words and images for email greetings, and for lines of products like mugs, posters, pillows, and balloons.

Bonnie Neubauer, a freelance writer in Pennsylvania, has tapped into the business-to-business greeting card niche. "[These cards] are tools to help sales people," Neubauer explains. "They help businesspeople keep in touch." She sells her ideas to a small company called IntroKnocks Business Greetings. Many other greeting card companies are getting into business-to-business cards, such as Hallmark. "So many people communicate through faxes, emails, and voicemail," Neubauer says, "that when a card comes in a colored envelope, with a handwritten address, it gets attention."

To spark ideas, Neubauer reads industry trade magazines, visits company Web sites, and looks over books of stock photos. Once she recognizes a business need, she comes up with a card to meet the need. "Some people only send out cartoons," she says about the business-to-business greeting card marketplace, "while others are more serious and only want cards with sophisticated photographs."

Working from home offices, greeting card writers and designers come up with their ideas, then submit them to the companies for consideration. "Coming up with good card ideas," Neubauer says, "involves taking clichés, and combining them with a tad of humor." Artists and photographers submit reproductions of their work, rather than their originals, because some companies don't return unaccepted submissions or may lose the submissions in the review process. Artists submit prints, color copies, duplicate transparencies, or CDs. Writers submit their ideas on index cards.

REQUIREMENTS

High School
Hone your writing and artistic skills in high school by taking English and art classes. Since many designers use computers to create their designs, computer science courses also will be helpful.

Postsecondary Training

College education is not necessary for freelancing as an artist and writer, though card companies looking to hire you for a full-time staff position may require a background in English, creative writing, graphic design, or commercial arts. Even if you only want to freelance, community college courses that instruct you in the use of computer design programs can help you to create professional-looking images for submission to companies.

Certification or Licensing

No certification program exists for greeting card writers or designers. However, if you decide to print your own cards and sell them to stores and representatives, you may be required by your state to maintain a business license.

Other Requirements

"I'm extremely self-motivated and grossly optimistic," Bonnie Neubauer says, in regard to making her home business a success. As for

Greeting Card Facts

- Consumers in the U.S. buy approximately seven billion greeting cards annually.
- The average household purchases 30 cards annually.
- The average person receives 20 cards each year.
- More than 100,000 retail outlets sell greeting cards.
- Women buy more than 80 percent of greeting cards.
- The most popular Everyday cards: Birthday (60 percent), Anniversary (8 percent), Get Well (7 percent), Friendship (6 percent), and Sympathy (6 percent).
- The most popular Seasonal cards: Christmas (60 percent), Valentine's Day (25 percent), Mother's Day (4 percent), Father's Day (3 percent), and Easter (3 percent).
- About 500 million e-cards are sent throughout the world each year.
- Despite the popularity of e-cards, consumers surveyed by the Greeting Card Association report that they still prefer a traditional card in most instances.

Source: Greeting Card Association

the writing itself, Neubauer emphasizes the importance of a sense of humor. "I love word-play," she says, "and I love marketing and promotions." Any writer and designer should also be patient, persistent, and capable of accepting rejection.

EXPLORING

Try writing and designing your own greeting cards. There are many software programs that will help you create attractive cards, stationery, and newsletters. Ask your high school English teacher or counselor to set up an interview with a greeting card designer or freelance writer.

EMPLOYERS

As a freelancer, you can work anywhere in the country and submit your work through the mail. *Artist's & Graphic Designer's Market* and *Writer's Market,* reference books published annually by Writer's Digest Books (http://www.writersdigest.com), include sections listing the greeting card companies that accept submissions from freelance artists and writers. While some companies only buy a few ideas a year, others buy hundreds of ideas. Hallmark, by far the largest greeting card manufacturer, doesn't accept unsolicited ideas, but hires many creative people for full-time staff positions. However, because of Hallmark's reputation as a great employer, competition for those positions is high.

STARTING OUT

Get to know the market by visiting local card shops; find out what's popular, and what kinds of cards each company sells. Visit the Web sites of the greeting card companies listed in *Artist's & Graphic Designer's Market* and *Writer's Market* and study their online catalogs. Most companies have very specific guidelines; one may publish only humorous cards, while another may only publish inspirational poems. Once you have a good sense of what companies are looking for, contact manufacturers, find out their submission guidelines, and submit samples of your work.

Another opportunity to break into the industry is through an internship. Every year, Hallmark holds a competition for their writing and editing internships. (See its contact information at the end of this article.)

ADVANCEMENT

After you've submitted a lot of your work to many different companies, you'll begin to make connections with people in the business. These connections can be valuable, leading you to jobs with better pay (such as royalties and percentages) and exclusive contracts. As you get to know the business better, you may choose to produce and market your own line of cards.

EARNINGS

Salaries vary widely among freelance greeting card writers and designers. Some card designers and writers sell only a few ideas a year. Others make a great deal of money, working exclusively with a company, or by manufacturing and distributing their own lines of cards and products. Card companies typically pay freelancers fees for each idea they buy. Some manufacturers may offer a royalty payment plan, including an initial advance. A small company may pay as little as $15 for an idea, while a larger company may pay $150 or more.

According to the U.S. Department of Labor, graphic designers earned a median annual salary of $41,280 in 2007, but pay ranged from less than $25,090 to more than $72,230. Writers of all types earned a median salary of $50,660 in 2007. The lowest 10 percent earned less than $26,530 while the highest paid writers earned more than $99,910 a year.

Greeting card designers and writers who work for a company usually receive benefits such as vacation days, sick leave, health and life insurance, and a savings and pension program. Self-employed designers and editors must provide their own benefits.

WORK ENVIRONMENT

Both writers and designers spend most of their time in an office, whether at home or in a company's space. Much of their work is done on a computer, whether they are designing images or writing copy. However, coming up with the initial ideas may involve a more creative routine. Many artists have certain activities that inspire them, such as listening to music, looking at photography and art books, or reading a novel.

OUTLOOK

According to the Greeting Card Association (GCA), the greeting card industry's retail sales have increased steadily from $2.1 billion in 1980, to more than $7.5 billion today. From designing animated email messages to greeting card CD-ROM programs, greeting card writers and designers will likely find more and more outlets for their work. Advances in Web technology should also aid the card designer in posting his or her ideas and images online to invite companies to browse, download, and purchase ideas.

Average growth is expected for this career in coming years. Despite the growing popularity of email, e-cards, and other communications technology, the GCA says the industry will not be adversely affected. E-cards are not as personal as standard greeting cards, nor are they appropriate for many situations, such as weddings, anniversaries, or for expressing sympathy. "Although email, text messaging and phone calls are valued by Americans for helping them communicate with family and friends, the majority of Americans say they prefer the old-fashioned handwritten card or letter to make someone feel truly special," the GCA says.

FOR MORE INFORMATION

For information on the industry and artist and writer guidelines, check out the following Web site:
Greeting Card Association
1156 15th Street, NW, Suite 900
Washington, DC 20005-1717
Tel: 202-393-1778
Email: info@greetingcard.org
http://www.greetingcard.org

For information on Hallmark's internship program and career opportunities, visit
Hallmark Cards Inc.
http://www.hallmark.com

Visit your library or bookstore for a copy of the latest edition of Writer's Market *and* Artist's & Graphic Designer's Market, *or contact*
Writer's Digest Books
http://www.writersdigest.com

INTERVIEW

Sandra Miller-Louden, from Salisbury, Pennsylvania, has been a greeting card writer since 1986. Her Web site, http://www.greeting cardwriting.com, is the only one exclusively devoted to the subject of greeting card writing. Sandra has written two books and has helped many people fulfill their writing dreams. She discussed her career with the editors of Careers in Focus: Entrepreneurs.

Q. Why did you decide to become a greeting card writer?

A. I've always loved greeting cards. I like buying and sending them; I love to receive them. I have always admired the way a great visual could interact with equally compelling words—whether serious or funny—to commiserate, commemorate, congratulate! I wanted to be a part of the world of greeting cards and since I can't draw worth a fig, my option was to write them.

Q. What are the main responsibilities of your job?

A. I write the words that go into greeting cards. Since I'm a freelance greeting card writer (as opposed to a staff or "in-house" writer), I work for many different companies. Many times, companies will send artwork to me—either drawn or photographed—and I must provide the verse to go with it. At other times, I create the entire concept—both visual and verse; however (to dispel one of the major myths about greeting card writing), I don't have to draw the visual—I describe it.

Q. What is your typical work day like? Do you interact with many people, whether in person or over the phone/ email?

A. My job is completely flexible and no two days—or nights—are the same. (You'll often find me working at 3:00 A.M. if that's when my ideas are flowing). I start by reviewing any approaching deadlines; greeting cards are basically divided into two categories: everyday and seasonal. Depending upon my assignment, I may be writing verses for Thanksgiving in May or Valentine's Day in October. As far as interacting with other people, I often say that 99 percent of all people I "know" in the industry I've never met face to face. I call them my "phone, fax, email, or blog people." These include editors, writers, artists, and cartoonists across the country and around the world. Writing, especially freelance writing, is often a solitary life.

Q. Can you describe your work environment?

A. Well, right now I'm still unpacking from a recent move, so stuff is piled up everywhere—which really isn't conducive to "working smart." However, I have a very friendly work environment surrounded by pictures and mementos I cherish. I often play music in the background and share my space with my cats,

Jenkins and Cinders. My work environment is a haven for me and I'm at my creative best while in it.

Q. **What do you like most and least about your job?**

A. I want to stress that my "worst days" in this job are better than my "best days" in other jobs I've had. What I love best about this job, is of course the writing and being able to create words that I know strangers will "adopt" as their own to send to people they care about and love. My words are present at all of life's basic events, and that makes me very happy. Also, I've received cards sent by people and when I turn the card over, the "written by" will sometimes be by one of my students. That's really a thrill.

What I like least about my job are overlapping deadlines; the busier I become, the more this happens. Luckily, I tend to be highly creative when under pressure, but that, too, has its downside because once the assignment is finished, I tend to be drained for a day or two. I also dislike the clerical side of my job. Since I do it all, I'm responsible for filing, invoicing, keeping office supplies, keeping receipts for taxes, following up on Web site content, etc. At some point soon, I'll need a part-time secretary, but as anyone who's started a business will tell you, giving up duties and delegating them is difficult.

Q. **What were your expectations entering the field? Were they much different from the realities?**

A. I started in 1986 writing verses on my dining room table, using my Smith-Corona typewriter—the same typewriter I used in college in 1972. I hoped to make some extra money writing greeting cards; I had always wanted to be a writer, yet with two small children, it was impossible to concentrate on longer works. As I continued to write cards, I tried to find more information on the subject, but there was very little available. It was a genre that was almost completely ignored, and the information that was out there did not reflect my experiences. I began putting together a course that I later taught at a local community college. As the years passed, others became very interested in my work and I was asked to do interviews, first locally, then nationally. I never expected the positive attention I received. Also, I never expected that there were so many people who would contact me to help make their creative dreams become a reality. Another aspect that has also morphed from my writing has been an active greeting card consultation service. I help new companies to accurately identify their creative niche and then fulfill that niche with appropriate artwork, verses, and occasions.

Q. **What kind of training did you receive for this position? What did you study in college? Did your education prepare you for this position?**

A. I received no specific training for this position. In college, I had a dual major—Spanish and English. However, from the beginning, I've always loved the written word and am totally fascinated with languages and how people use words to communicate. One of my most vivid memories is sitting down at my mother's manual Underwood typewriter and teaching myself how to type by copying sentences from a book I was reading—I absolutely loved the feel of keys under my fingers, as they made words on a sheet of paper. I was fortunate to have very supportive English and Spanish professors both in high school and college who encouraged me to write. I remember in 10th grade, my English teacher wrote on a short story I'd turned in: "Very good, as usual." I think the writing seeds were always there; this single comment started them blooming.

Q. **Did you complete any internships to help you prepare for your career?**

A. No, I never completed any internships. In fact, the first time I submitted a batch of greeting card verses to an editor, I didn't even know enough to mark my envelope, "ATTN: EDITORIAL." Again, though, just as with my sophomore English teacher, the very first batch I sent came back to me with a handwritten note from the editor that said: "Very close. Please feel free to try again." Those eight encouraging words were enough to have me dig in my heels and keep trying. Within three months, I'd sold my first greeting card verse. After that, I learned on my own from my own mistakes and also from asking questions. I'd call editors and ask them what they were looking for and what separated good copy from inadequate writing. I tell my students and readers that my first four years in this business were all about making mistakes, learning from those mistakes and moving past them. I kid them by saying I save people four years by pointing out errors I made so they won't have to repeat those same mistakes.

Q. **What is the best way to find a job in this field?**

A. It's really pretty simple. First, read as many greeting cards as you possibly can. Just stand there and read card after card, not only the traditional rhymed metered verse, but what I've termed "contemporary prose"—the soft, conversational, nonrhyming verse—and of course humor, which is something most editors want today. Don't just think Hallmark or American Greetings; it's tough to break into these companies. Most people don't realize there are many greeting card companies in the United States and Canada. Most of these are solid mid-size and smaller companies that encourage freelance writers and artists. Do an Internet search for greeting card companies; many of them have their creative guidelines posted right on their sites. Then come up with some solid ideas and begin submitting them to an editor. When I speak at career days in high schools, students are always amazed that there is no minimum age limit for a freelance greeting card writer. As long as you have a Social Security number, you can send in verses. There are certain formats and rules concerning how to submit; these are often covered in the set of guidelines issued from the company.

Q. What are the most important skills and personal qualities for someone in your career?

A. First, you have to love language. You have to be fascinated with the multitude of expressions, phrases, synonyms, and figurative meanings that populate a language. You should also be a visual person; you should have an eye for what stands out in a picture and be able to build a verse around that picture. For example, if I show you a photograph of three Dalmatian puppies, you might focus on their spots and write something like: "I knew you were cute the minute I spotted you." Second, you have to "write tight." There is no place in greeting card writing for long, drawn-out metaphors or obscure references. Finally, you must have empathy for human relationships and understand how and why people need to communicate their emotions. Greeting cards are sent at life's most important milestones, whether a birth, anniversary, wedding, graduation, promotion, new home, retirement, death, as well as the many holidays people celebrate: Mother's and Father's Day, Valentine's, Easter, Passover, Christmas, Hanukkah, Kwanzaa, Thanksgiving, etc. As a greeting card writer, you must tap into these occasions and get a real feeling for them. You may not have a daughter, for example, but you must be able to think "daughter thoughts" to write a successful card that would be sent to someone's daughter.

Q. What advice would you give to someone who is interested in pursuing this type of career?

A. I generally give a one-word piece of advice about writing: Write. There are many people out there who enjoy "talking about writing," but who never sit down at the keyboard and just write. They also equate having a computer, fax, printer, etc. with writing success. I point out to them that while these machines are certainly extremely valuable, if I had the choice between having a computer, fax, and printer or having imagination, tenacity, and discipline, guess which trio I'd pick? It doesn't mean the two sets are mutually exclusive, by any means. What it does mean is, simply, don't fall in the habit of equating expensive trappings with writing. Don't get into the mind set that "if I only had a bigger, better, faster computer, I'd be a bigger, better, faster writer."

Q. What is the future employment outlook in the field?

A. Well, let me start by saying that about seven to eight years ago, many people were worried about e-cards taking over traditional paper cards—I'd get asked that question constantly in interviews. Today, no one asks me that question because what I said back then has come to pass. E-cards and paper cards can and will coexist peacefully. The card industry, like many other industries, has changed over the years. Some smaller companies have been purchased by bigger ones; in most cases, however, the creative or editorial side of the takeover hasn't been affected. Knowing where and how to look for opportunities is part of what I teach and what I delve into in my book—as long as people continue to use a greeting card to mark all of life's many important occasions, there will be a need for writers to come up with the verses. Remember, people will pick a greeting card up for its visual—but if the words are all wrong, back that card will go on the rack until just the right words are found.

Information Brokers

OVERVIEW

Information brokers, sometimes called *online researchers* or *independent information professionals,* compile information from online databases and services. They work for clients in a number of different professions, researching marketing surveys, newspaper articles, business and government statistics, abstracts, and other sources of information. They prepare reports and presentations based on their research. Information brokers have home-based operations, or they work full-time for libraries, law offices, government agencies, and corporations.

HISTORY

Strange as it may seem, some of the earliest examples of online researchers are the keepers of a library established by Ptolemy I in Egypt in the 3rd century B.C. These librarians helped to build the first great library by copying and revising classical Greek texts. The monks of Europe also performed some of the modern-day researcher's tasks by building libraries and printing books. Despite their great efforts, libraries weren't used extensively until the 18th century, when literacy increased among the general population. In 1803, the first public library in the United States opened in Connecticut.

In the late 1800s and early 1900s, many different kinds of library associations evolved, reflecting the number of special libraries already established (such as medical and law libraries). With all the developments of the 20th century, these library associations helped to promote special systems and tools for locating information. These systems eventually developed into the online databases and Internet search engines used today. The Internet, although created in 1969

QUICK FACTS

School Subjects
Computer science
English
Journalism

Personal Skills
Communication/ideas
Technical/scientific

Work Environment
Primarily indoors
Primarily one location

Minimum Education Level
Bachelor's degree

Salary Range
$20,000 to $64,000 to $100,000+

Certification or Licensing
None available

Outlook
Faster than the average

DOT
N/A

GOE
N/A

NOC
N/A

O*NET-SOC
N/A

and subsidized by the government as a communication system for the Department of Defense, didn't become a significant source of information until relaxed government policies allowed for its commercial use in 1991.

THE JOB

An interest in the Internet and computer skills are important to success as an independent information broker, but this specialist needs to understand much more than just search engines. Information brokers need to master Dialog, LexisNexis, and other information databases. They also have to compile information by using fax machines, photocopiers, and telephones, as well as by conducting personal interviews. If you think this sounds like the work of a private eye, you are not far off; as a matter of fact, some information brokers have worked as private investigators.

A majority of research projects, however, are marketing based. Suppose a company wants to embark on a new, risky venture— maybe a fruit distribution company wants to make figs as popular as apples and oranges. First, the company's leaders might want to know some basic information about fig consumption. How many people have even eaten a fig? What articles about figs have been published in national magazines? What have been recent annual sales of figs, Fig Newtons, and other fig-based treats? What popular recipes include figs? The company hires consultants, marketing experts, and researchers to gather all this information.

Each researcher has his or her own approach to accomplishing tasks, but every researcher must first get to know the subject. A researcher who specializes in retail and distribution might already be familiar with the trade associations, publications, and other sources of industry information. Another researcher might have to learn as much as possible, as quickly as possible, about the lingo and organizations involved with the fruit distribution industry. This includes using the Internet's basic search engines to get a sense of what kind of information is available. The researcher then uses a database service, such as the Dialog system, which makes available billions of pages of text and images, including complete newspaper and magazine articles, wire service stories, and company profiles. Because database services often charge the user for the time spent searching or documents viewed, online researchers must know all the various tips and commands for efficient searching. Once the search is complete, and they've downloaded the information needed, online researchers must prepare the information for the company. They may be expected to make a presentation to the company or write a complete report that includes pie charts, graphs, and other illustrations to accompany the text.

The legal profession hires information brokers to search cases, statutes, and other sources of law; update law library collections; and locate data to support cases, such as finding expert witnesses, or researching the history of the development of a defective product that caused personal injury. The health care industry needs information brokers to gather information on drugs, treatments, devices, illnesses, or clinical trials. An information broker who specializes in public records researches personal records (such as birth, death, marriage, adoption, and criminal records), corporations, and property ownership. Other industries that rely on information brokers include banking and finance, government and public policy, and science and technology.

"This isn't the kind of profession you can do right out of high school or college," says Mary Ellen Bates, an independent information professional based in Niwot, Colorado. "It requires expertise in searching the professional online services. You can't learn them on your own time; you have to have real-world experience as an online researcher. Many of the most successful information brokers are former librarians." Her success in the business has led her to serve as past president of the Association of Independent Information Professionals, to write and publish articles about the business, and to serve as a consultant to libraries and other organizations. Some of her projects have included research on the market for independent living facilities for senior citizens and the impact of large grocery chains on independent grocery stores. She's also been asked to find out what rental car companies do with cars after they're past their prime. "Keep in mind that you need a lot more than Internet research skills," Bates says. "You need the ability to run your business from the top to bottom. That means accounting, marketing, collections, strategic planning, and personnel management."

The expense of the commercial database services has affected the career of another online researcher, Sue Carver of Richland, Washington. Changes in Dialog's usage rates have forced her to seek out other ways to use her library skills. In addition to such services as market research and document delivery, Carver's Web page promotes a book-finding service, helping people to locate collectible and out-of-print books. "I have found this a fun, if not highly lucrative, activity which puts me in contact with a wide variety of people," she says. "This is a case where the Internet opens the door to other possibilities. Much of this business is repackaging information in a form people want to buy. This is limited only by your imagination." But she also emphasizes that the job of online researcher requires highly specialized skills in information retrieval. "Nonlibrarians often do not appreciate the vast array of reference material that existed before the Internet," she says, "nor how much librarians have contributed to the information age." Carver holds a master's degree in library science and has worked as a reference librarian, which involved her with searches on patents, molecular biology, and other technical subjects. She has also worked as an indexer on a nuclear engineering project and helped plan a search and retrieval system on a separate nuclear project.

REQUIREMENTS

High School

Take computer classes that teach word and data processing programs, presentation programs, and how to use Internet search engines. Any class offered by your high school or public library on information retrieval will familiarize you with database searches and such services as Dialog, LexisNexis, and Dow Jones. English and composition courses will teach you to organize information and write clearly. Speech and theater classes will help you develop the skills to give presentations in front of clients. Journalism classes and working on your high school newspaper will involve you directly in information retrieval and writing.

Postsecondary Training

It is recommended that you start with a good liberal arts program in a college or university, then pursue a master's degree in either a subject specialty or in library and information science. Developing expertise in a particular subject will prepare you for a specialty in information brokering.

Many online researchers have master's degrees in library science. The American Library Association accredits library and information science programs and offers a number of scholarships. Courses in library programs deal with techniques of data collection and analysis, use of graphical presentation of sound and text, and networking and telecommunications. Internships are also available in some library science programs.

Continuing education courses are important for online researchers with advanced degrees. Because of the rapidly changing technology, researchers need to attend seminars and take courses through such organizations as the Special Libraries Association. Many online researchers take additional courses in their subject matter specialization. Mary Ellen Bates attends meetings of the Society of Competitive Intelligence Professionals (http://www.scip.org), since a lot of her work is in the field of competitive intelligence.

Other Requirements

In addition to all the varied computer skills necessary to succeed as an information broker, you must have good communication skills. "You're marketing all the time," Bates says. "If you're not comfortable marketing yourself and speaking publicly, you'll never make it in this business." To keep your business running, you need persistence to pursue new clients and sources of information. You are your own boss, so you have to be self-motivated to meet deadlines. Good record-keeping skills will help you manage the financial details of the business and help you keep track of contacts.

Sue Carver advises that you keep up on current events and pay close attention to detail. You should welcome the challenge of locating hard-to-find facts and articles. "I have a logical mind," Carver says, "and love puzzles and mysteries."

EXPLORING

If you've ever had to write an extensive research paper, then you've probably already had experience with online research. In college, many of your term papers will require that you become familiar with Lexis/Nexis and other library systems. The reference librarians of your school and public libraries should be happy to introduce you to the various library tools available. On the Internet, experiment with the search engines; each service has slightly different features and capabilities.

Visit Mary Ellen Bates' Web site at http://www.batesinfo.com for extensive information about the business and to read articles she's written. She's also the coauthor of a number of books, including *Building and Running a Successful Research Business: A Guide For the Independent Information Professional* (Information Today Inc., 2003), *Super Searchers Cover the World: The Online Secrets of International Business Researchers* (Information Today Inc., 2001), and *Researching Online For Dummies*, 2nd ed. (Hungry Minds, 2000).

EMPLOYERS

A large number of information professionals are employed by colleges, universities, and corporations, and gain experience in full-time staff positions before starting their own businesses. Those who work for themselves contract with a number of different kinds of businesses and organizations. People seeking marketing information make the most use of the services of information professionals. Attorneys, consulting firms, public relations firms, government agencies, and private investigators also hire researchers. With the Internet, a researcher can work anywhere in the country, serving clients all around the world. However, living in a large city will allow an online researcher better access to more expansive public records when performing manual research.

STARTING OUT

People become researchers through a variety of different routes. They may go into business for themselves after gaining a lot of experience within an industry, such as in aviation or pharmaceuticals. Using their expertise, insider knowledge, and professional connections, they can serve as a consultant on issues affecting the business. Or they may become an independent researcher after working as a special librarian, having developed computer and search skills. The one thing most researchers have in common, however, is extensive experience in finding information and presenting it. Once they have the knowledge necessary to start their own information business, online researchers should take seminars offered by professional organizations. Amelia Kassel, president and owner of MarketingBase (http://www.marketing base.com), a successful information brokering company, offers a mentoring program via email. As mentor, she advises on such subjects as online databases, marketing strategies, and pricing.

Before leaving her full-time job, Mary Ellen Bates spent a year preparing to start her own business. She says, "I didn't want to spend time doing start-up stuff that I could spend marketing or doing paying work." She saved business cards and established contacts. She saved $10,000 and set up a home-based office with a computer, desk, office supplies, fax, and additional phone lines. To help others starting out, Bates has written *Getting Your First Five Clients,* available through the Association of Independent Information Professionals.

ADVANCEMENT

The first few years of any business are difficult and require long hours of marketing, promotion, and building a clientele. Advancement will depend on the online researcher's ability to make connections and to broaden their client base. Some researchers start out specializing in a particular area, such as in telephone research or public record research, before venturing out into different areas. Once they're capable of handling projects from diverse sources, they can expand their business. They can also take on larger projects as they begin to meet other reliable researchers with whom they can join forces.

EARNINGS

Even if they have a great deal of research experience, self-employed information brokers' first few years in the business may be lean ones, and they should expect to make as little as $20,000. As with any small business, it takes a few years to develop contacts and establish a reputation for quality work. Independent information brokers usually charge between $45 and $100 an hour, depending on the project. Eventually, an online researcher should be able to make a salary equivalent to that of a full-time special librarian—a 2007 salary survey by the Special Libraries Association puts the national median at $64,000. Some very experienced independent researchers with a number of years of self-employment may make well over $100,000.

Helen Burwell, president of Burwell Enterprises, estimates that the average information broker charges $75 an hour. This hourly rate is affected by factors such as geographic location and the broker's knowledge of the subject matter. Information brokers can make more money in cities like New York and Washington, D.C., where their services are in higher demand. Also, someone doing high-level patent research, which requires a great deal of expertise, can charge more than someone retrieving public records.

Information brokers who work full time for companies earn salaries comparable to other information technology (IT) professionals. Salaries for IT professionals can range from $36,000 for entry-level personnel to more than $90,000 for those with more than 10 years' experience. A full-time information broker who works for a large corporation primarily in the area of competitive intelligence can earn $100,000 annually.

Benefits for full-time workers include vacation and sick time, health, and sometimes dental, insurance, and pension or 401(k) plans. Self-employed information brokers must provide their own benefits.

WORK ENVIRONMENT

Most independent researchers work out of their own homes. This means they have a lot of control over their environment, but it also means they're always close to their workstations. As a result, online researchers may find themselves working longer hours than if they had an outside office and a set weekly schedule. "This is easily a 50- to 60-hour a week job," Mary Ellen Bates says. Online researchers are their own bosses, but they may work as a member of a team with other researchers and consultants on some projects. They will also need to discuss the project with their clients both before and after they've begun their research.

Information brokers employed by companies work in an office environment. Although most of their work takes place at a computer, they may have to make trips to libraries, government offices, and other places that hold information that's not available online. Whether self-employed or not, information brokers spend some time in board rooms and conference situations making presentations of their findings.

OUTLOOK

Helen Burwell anticipates that independent information professionals will continue to find a great deal of work, but the growth of the industry won't be as rapid as in the past because of the increasing number of new information science graduates entering the field.

The Internet is making it easier for people and businesses to conduct their own online research; this is expected to help business for online researchers rather than hurt. Alex Kramer, past president of the Association of Independent Information Professionals, predicts that the more people recognize the vast amount of information available to them, the more they'll seek out the assistance of online researchers to efficiently compile that information. There will be continuing demand for information brokers in marketing, competitive intelligence, legal research, and science and technology.

Employment experts predict that with the growing reliance on computer technology, businesses will be willing to pay top dollar for employees and consultants who are flexible, mobile, and able to navigate the technology with ease.

FOR MORE INFORMATION

For information about library science programs and scholarships, contact

American Library Association
50 East Huron
Chicago, IL 60611-2729
Tel: 800-545-2433
http://www.ala.org

For information on information science careers, contact
American Society for Information Science and Technology
1320 Fenwick Lane, Suite 510
Silver Spring, MD 20910-3560
Tel: 301-495-0900
Email: asis@asis.org
http://www.asis.org

To learn more about the career of information broker, contact
Association of Independent Information Professionals
8550 United Plaza Boulevard, Suite 1001
Baton Rouge, LA 70809-0200
Tel: 225-408-4400
Email: office@aiip.org
http://www.aiip.org

For information on earnings and continuing education, contact
Special Libraries Association
331 South Patrick Street
Alexandria, VA 22314-3501
Tel: 703-647-4900
Email: sla@sla.org
http://www.sla.org

Internet Consultants

QUICK FACTS

School Subjects
Business
Computer science

Personal Skills
Communication/ideas
Technical/scientific

Work Environment
Primarily indoors
Primarily multiple
    locations

Minimum Education Level
Bachelor's degree

Salary Range
$35,000 to $65,000 to
    $100,000+

Certification or Licensing
Voluntary

Outlook
Faster than the average

DOT
N/A

GOE
N/A

NOC
N/A

O*NET-SOC
N/A

OVERVIEW

Internet consultants use their technological and computer skills to help people or businesses access and utilize the Internet. Their work may include implementing or refining a networking system, creating a Web site, establishing an online ordering or product support system, or training employees to maintain and update their newly established Web site. Some consultants work independently, and others may be employed by a consulting agency.

HISTORY

The Internet as we know it has only been around a little longer than a decade. In this short amount of time, the Internet has brought new ways of communicating and selling products and services to customers, without the presence of an actual store or office. With the fast growth of Internet sales and services, companies with a Web presence need people who can help create and manage sites to fit the company's business goals. This created the need for the Internet consultant. Because of constantly evolving technology, the future will require even more specialized and complex skills of Internet consultants.

THE JOB

The job of an Internet consultant can vary from day to day and project to project. Duties can also vary depending on the consultant's areas of expertise. For example, an Internet consultant specializing in creative work may design a Web site and help a company create a consistent visual message, while a consultant who is a "techie" may get involved with setting up the company's intranet or Internet connections. The entrepreneurial Internet consultant may help a business establish an online storefront and an online ordering and processing system. Some Internet consultants who have considerable business experience may work with CEOs or other company heads to analyze the company's current use of the Internet and determine what markets the company is reaching.

Some consultants work independently (running their own businesses) and are paid for their work by the hour; others may be paid by the project. Those who work for consulting firms may be salaried employees of the firm. Some businesses may require that the consultants be on-site; this means that they work on a particular project at the company's office for several days, weeks, or months. Many consultants work out of their home offices and only visit the company occasionally such as when meetings are necessary.

Frank Smith, an Internet consultant in San Diego, California, started working in this career, because, as he puts it, "I was essentially a computer geek and a technology freak. I was interested in computer technology early on and just continued to learn." Smith has a degree in business administration and was previously employed as a project manager for a manufacturing firm. The appeal of working at different locations, meeting a variety of technological challenges, and working independently, however, enticed him into the field of consulting, as it does many people. Smith added to his computer knowledge by learning many software programs and programming languages. He also took classes that focused on special elements of Web site design, networking, and image manipulation. Internet consultants must constantly update their knowledge to keep abreast of new technological developments.

Smith says it's not difficult to love his job because there are no typical days and no typical projects. "I may work with a company to develop their Web presence, or I may simply analyze what they are currently doing and give them some tips to make their Internet and networking connections more efficient." One of the first things a consultant may do on a new project for a business is to meet with key people at the company. During the meeting the consultant gathers information on the business and finds out what the company hopes to do through the Internet. "I don't simply design a Web site and get them on the Internet," emphasizes Smith. "I get a feel for their company and their business. I look at their current marketing, advertising, and sales material and make sure their Web site will be consistent with their printed material."

This means the consultant's work involves researching, analyzing information, and preparing reports based on their findings. As Smith notes, "This takes time and research. Sometimes I go home from a meeting with a stack of material about the company, and I study it to make sure I am familiar with the company and its focus." Internet consultants must know their clients to be successful. Smith adds, "I believe this is an important business aspect that is sometimes overlooked by consultants and company executives when they go on the Internet."

Internet consultants may also develop the entire Internet setup, including the hardware and software, for their client. The client may be a company that is upgrading its equipment or a company that has never been connected to the Internet before. Some consultants also train company employees to monitor, maintain, and enhance their Web site.

According to Smith, consultants who have business experience and business degrees, as well as some technical training, will be the most highly sought. "A good consultant needs to have a working knowledge of the business world as well as computer and technological expertise." The consultant with an understanding of business is able to offer clients more thorough service than the consultant who is only a computer whiz. "Many consultants can put together a Web site for their clients," Smith explains, "however, more and more companies are beginning to look for the consultant who can offer added value, such as business analysis or marketing skills that will enhance their business and its products and services."

Although Smith feels there is currently an abundance of work for Internet consultants, he believes that demand may slow as companies get connected to the Internet and establish their presence. New technologies, however, are constantly being developed. The consultant who keeps up with technical changes will be able to offer new and old clients improved and different services.

Some people may use their computer skills to work as consultants in a sideline business or as a supplement to their part-time or full-time job. Linda McNamara is employed on a part-time basis as a Web site designer with a government agency in Illinois. In addition to that job, though, she also works as an independent Internet consultant. McNamara partners with another consultant to operate a business that designs and maintains Web sites for small enterprises in the area.

Although McNamara does not consult on the large scale that Smith does, she, too, emphasizes that consultants need to have good communication skills. "Everyone has a different idea of how they want their Web site to look," she says. "This requires that I have the ability to listen, communicate, and perform according to expectations."

REQUIREMENTS

High School

If you are considering a career as an Internet consultant, you should take a general high school curriculum that is college preparatory. Make sure you take computer science and business courses. You should also take courses that develop your analytical and problem-solving skills such as mathematics (including algebra and geometry) and sciences (including chemistry and physics). Take English courses to develop the research and communication skills you'll need for this profession.

Postsecondary Training

While a college degree may not be necessary to gain entry into this field, you will find it easier to get the best jobs and advance if you have one. As the high-tech market tightens and becomes more sophisticated, consultants with degrees generally have more opportunities than those with a high school diploma. Some people enter the field with computer- or e-commerce–related degrees; others have a liberal arts or business background that includes computer studies. No matter what your major, though, you should take plenty of computer classes, study programming, and play on the Web.

Because consultants are usually responsible for marketing themselves, you should have good business skills and knowledge of marketing and sales, as well as computer knowledge. Therefore, take business and management classes, as well as economics and marketing. The consultant with a broad educational background may have the inside edge in certain situations. More and more clients are looking for consultants who can offer "value-added" services such as business analysis and marketing assistance along with computer skills. As one consultant says, "Just attending college teaches rigorous, valuable lessons that can benefit you and your clients in the real world."

Certification or Licensing

There are numerous certifications and designations available in programming languages, software, and network administration. Some employers may require that consultants have certain certifications. To become certified, you will probably have to complete a training course and pass a written exam. Often the company that puts out a new technology, such as new software, will sponsor a training program.

The Institute for Certification of Computing Professionals offers the certified computing professional and the associate computing professional designations, as well as other designations for different professionals in information technology. To become certified, you must pass various written exams and fulfill certain work experience requirements.

Other Requirements

Internet consultants must be lifelong learners. You should have the desire and initiative to keep up with new technology, software, and hardware. You must also have good communication skills, including good listening skills. Creativity and a good eye for graphic design are also desirable. Because Internet consultants deal with many different people in various lines of work, they must be flexible and have good interpersonal skills. To be a successful consultant, you should be self-motivated and have the ability to work alone as well as with groups. You also need to have the patience and perseverance to see projects through.

EXPLORING

You can explore your interest in computers by getting involved with a computer users group or club in your community or school. If a computer trade show comes to your area, be sure to attend. You'll be able to see new advances in technology and talk with others interested in this field. Search the Web for interesting sites, and look at their source code to see how they were developed. Increase your knowledge by experimenting and learning independently. Check out library books about computers and teach yourself some programming or Web site design skills. Mastering a Web page authoring program is a good introduction to Web design.

Offer to help people you know set up their home computer systems or do upgrades. Gain experience working with people by volunteering to help seniors or others learn how to use computers at a community center. Try to get a summer or part-time job at a computer store. Large retailers, such as Best Buy, also have computer departments where you might find work. The business experience will be beneficial, even if you are not working directly on the Internet.

By simply accessing the Internet frequently and observing different Web site designs and the increasing number of e-commerce sites, you can gain an insight into how rapidly the information technology industry is changing. Contact computer consultants, Web site designers, or programmers in your area and set up an information interview with them. At the interview you can ask them questions about their educational background, what they like about the work, how they market their business, what important skills someone wanting to enter the field should have, and any other things you are interested in knowing about this work.

EMPLOYERS

Many Internet consultants work independently, running their own consulting businesses. Others may be salaried employees of traditional management consulting firms that have Internet consulting divisions or departments. And still others may be salaried employees of Internet consulting companies.

Independent consultants have the added responsibility of marketing their services and always looking for new projects to work on. Consultants at a firm are typically assigned to work on certain projects.

Clients that hire Internet consultants include small businesses, large corporations, health care facilities, and government institutions. Consultants work all across the country (and world), but large cities may offer more job opportunities. Some consultants specialize in working with a certain type of business such as a hospital or a retail enterprise.

STARTING OUT

Most consultants enter the field by working for an established consulting firm. This way they can gain experience and develop a portfolio and a list of references before venturing out on their own as an independent consultant or moving to a different firm in a higher position. The Internet is a good resource to use to find employment. There are many sites that post job openings. Local employment agencies and newspapers and trade magazines also list job opportunities. In addition, your college's career services office should be able to help you.

Networking is a key element to becoming a successful consultant and requires getting in touch with previous business and social associates as well as making new contacts.

ADVANCEMENT

Internet consultants have several avenues for advancement. As they become known as experts in their field, the demand for their services will increase. This demand can support an increase in fees. They can also specialize in a certain aspect of computer consulting, which can increase their client base and fees. Those working for consulting firms may move into management or partner positions. Consultants who want to work independently can advance by starting their own consulting businesses. Eventually they may be able to hire consultants to work under them. Some consultants leave the field to head up the computer departments or perform Web site administration for corporations or other agencies. Because of the continuous developments within the information technology industry, the advancement possibilities for consultants who continually upgrade their knowledge and skills are practically endless.

EARNINGS

Internet consultants' earnings vary widely depending on their geographic location, type of work performed, and their experience and reputation. Beginning consultants may make around $35,000 per year, while many consultants earn around $65,000 annually. Some consultants have salaries that exceed $100,000 a year.

Many independent consultants charge by the hour, with fees ranging from $45 an hour to well above $100 an hour. Consultants who work on contract must estimate the hours needed to complete the project and their rate of pay when determining their contract price. Independent consultants must also realize that not all their work time is "billable," meaning that general office work, record keeping, billing, maintaining current client contacts, and seeking new business do not generate revenue. This nonbillable time must be factored into contract or hourly rates when determining annual income.

Although independent consultants may be able to generate good contract or hourly fees, they do not receive benefits that may be typical of salaried employees. For example, independent consultants are responsible for their own medical, disability, and life insurances. They do not receive vacation pay, and when they are not working, they are not generating income. Retirement plans must also be self-funded and self-directed.

WORK ENVIRONMENT

Internet consultants can expect to work in a variety of settings. Depending on the project, independent consultants may work out of their homes or private offices. At other times, they may be required to work on-site at the client's facilities, which may, for example, be a hospital, office building, or factory. Consultants employed by a large or small consulting firm may also spend time working at the consulting firm's offices or telecommuting from home.

Internet consultants generally can expect to work in a clean office environment. Consultants may work independently or as part of a team, depending on the project's requirements.

Consulting can be a very intense job that may require long hours to meet a project's deadline. Some settings where employees or consultants are driven by a strict deadline or where a project is not progressing as planned may be stressful. Many people in the computer field often work more than 40 hours a week and may need to work nights and weekends. In addition, Internet consultants must spend time keeping current with the latest technology by reading and researching. Intensive computer work can result in eye strain, hand and wrist injuries, and back pain.

OUTLOOK

There is currently a large demand for Internet consultants; however, as more and more companies become established on the Web, they may hire their own Webmasters and systems specialists. In addition, new software programs are making the development of simple Web pages easier to create without expert help.

Frank Smith notes, "If you don't stay on top of the industry, you quickly become unemployable. The market will mature, and companies will not be struggling to get their Web site up and running like they are now. Consultants will have to be more competent and offer more to their clients." Good consultants who keep current with technology and who are willing to learn and adapt should have plenty of job opportunities.

FOR MORE INFORMATION

This organization's Foundation for Information Technology Education offers a limited number of scholarships and has information on the tech industry. To learn more, contact
Association of Information Technology Professionals
401 North Michigan Avenue, Suite 2400
Chicago, IL 60611-4267
Tel: 800-224-9371
http://www.aitp.org or http://www.edfoundation.org

To learn more about consulting, contact
Independent Computer Consultants Association
11131 South Towne Square, Suite F
St. Louis, MO 63123-7817
Tel: 314-892-1675
Email: execdirector@icca.org
http://www.icca.org

For certification information, contact
Institute for Certification of Computing Professionals
2350 East Devon Avenue, Suite 115
Des Plaines, IL 60018-4610
Tel: 800-843-8227
Email: office@iccp.org
http://www.iccp.org

Internet Entrepreneurs

OVERVIEW

Internet entrepreneurs use the exciting technology of the Internet to sell products or services. They may research the marketability of a product or service, decide on what product or service to sell, organize their business, and set up their storefront on the Web. Numerous small business owners who sell a limited number of products or a specific service have found the Internet a great place to begin their business venture because start-up costs may be less than for traditional businesses.

HISTORY

The Internet became a popular sales tool in the 1990s, and continues to grow today. Although many dot-com companies failed in the early 2000s, Internet sales remain an integral part of our economy.

More and more revenue is generated online each year, and some Internet stores, such as Amazon.com, have had tremendous success in this field. As the Internet continues to grow in popularity and importance, more consumers will be exposed to Internet stores on a daily basis. This will create a strong demand for Internet entrepreneurs to research and market potential products and services, as well as manage businesses and employees.

THE JOB

Because of the vastness of the Internet, the role of an Internet entrepreneur can vary as much as the numerous Web sites on the Internet. Expert opinion on what makes one Web site or one business more successful than another differs, too. E-commerce is a new and relatively unexplored field for entrepreneurs. But, because most entrepreneurs have innovative and creative natures, this uncertainty and uncharted territory is what they love.

Like traditional entrepreneurs, Internet entrepreneurs must have strong business skills. They come up with ideas for an Internet product or service, research the feasibility of selling this product or service, decide what they need to charge to make a profit, determine how to advertise their business, and even arrange for financing for their business if necessary. In addition, Internet entrepreneurs typically have computer savvy and may even create and maintain their own sites.

Some entrepreneurs may choose to market a service, such as Web site design, to target the business-to-business market. Other Internet entrepreneurs may decide to market a service, such as computer dating, to target the individual consumer market. Still others may develop a "virtual store" on the Internet and sell products that target businesses or individual consumers.

Internet stores vary in size, items for sale, and the range of products. Smaller Internet stores, for example, may market the work done by a single craftsperson or businessperson. Many large Internet stores focus on selling a specific product or line of products. As some of these stores have grown they have diversified their merchandise. Amazon.com is one such example. Originally a small, online bookstore, the company now sells music CDs, videos, jewelry, toys and housewares, along with books. Other Internet stores, such as those of Eddie Bauer and Sears, may be extensions of catalog or traditional brick-and-mortar stores.

Many Internet businesses begin small, with one person working as the owner, manager, Webmaster, marketing director, and accountant, among other positions. John Axne of Chicago, Illinois, took on all these responsibilities when he developed his own one-person business designing Web sites for small companies and corporations. "Having my own business allows me more creative freedom," says Axne. The successful Internet entrepreneur, like the successful traditional entrepreneur, is often able to combine his or her interests with work to fill a niche in the business world. "It's a great fit for me," Axne explains. "I have a passion for computers and a love of learning. This business allows me to sell myself and my services." Dave Wright of Venice, California, is also an Internet entrepreneur and Web site designer. He, too, combined his interests with computer skills to start his business. "I had a strong interest in art," he says. "I simply married my art and graphic art experience with computers."

Those who want to start their own businesses on the Web must be very focused and self-motivated. Just like any other entrepreneur, they always need to keep an eye on the competition to see what products and services as well as prices and delivery times others offer. While Internet entrepreneurs do not need to be computer whizzes, they should enjoy learning about technology so that they can keep up with new developments that may help them with their businesses. Internet entrepreneurs must also be decision makers, and many are drawn to running their own businesses because of the control it offers. "I'm a control freak," Wright admits. "This way I can oversee every aspect of my job."

While the Internet world is appealing to many, there are risks for those who start their own businesses. "The Internet changes so rapidly that in five years it may be entirely different," Wright says. "That's why I started a business that simply sells services and didn't require a major investment. It is a business that I can get into and out of quickly if I find it necessary. There is no product, per se, and no inventory." Despite uncertainties, however, Web stores continue to open and the number of Internet entrepreneurs continues to grow.

REQUIREMENTS

High School

If you are considering becoming an Internet entrepreneur, there are a number of classes you can take in high school to help prepare you for these careers. Naturally you should take computer science courses to give you a familiarity with using computers and the Web. Business and marketing courses will also be beneficial for you. Also, take mathematics, accounting, or bookkeeping classes because, as an entrepreneur, you will be responsible for your company's finances. Take history classes to learn about economic trends and psychology classes to learn about human behavior. A lot of advertising and product promotion has a psychological element. Finally, take plenty of English classes. These classes will help you develop your communication skills—skills that will be vital to your work as a business owner.

Postsecondary Training

Although there are no specific educational requirements for Internet entrepreneurs, a college education will certainly enhance your skills and chances for success. Like anyone interested in working for or running a traditional business, take plenty of business, economics, and marketing and management classes. Your education should also include accounting or bookkeeping classes. Keep up with computer and Internet developments by taking computer classes. Some schools offer certificates and degrees in e-commerce. Many schools have undergraduate degree programs in business or business administration, but you can also enter this field with other degrees. Dave Wright, for example, graduated with a degree from art school, while John Axne has degrees in biomedical engineering and interactive media.

Certification or Licensing

While there are no specific certifications available for Internet entrepreneurs, professional associations such as the Institute for Certification of Computing Professionals and the Institute of Certified Professional Managers offer voluntary management-related certifications to industry professionals. These designations are helpful in proving your abilities to an employer or client. The more certifications you have, the more you have to offer.

Licenses may be required for running a business, depending on the type of business. Since requirements vary, you will need to check with local and state agencies for regulations in your area.

Other Requirements

Internet entrepreneurs must have the desire and initiative to keep up with new technology and business trends. Because they must deal with many different people in various lines of work, they need to be flexible problem solvers and have strong communication skills. Creativity and insight into new and different ways of doing business are qualities that are essential for an entrepreneur to be successful. In addition, because the Internet and e-commerce are relatively new and the future of Internet businesses is uncertain, those who enter the field are generally risk-takers and eager to be on the cutting edge of commerce and technology. Dave Wright notes, "This is not a job for someone looking for security. The Internet world is always changing. This is both exciting and scary to me as a businessperson. This is one career where you are not able to see where you will be in five years."

EXPLORING

There are numerous ways in which you can explore your interest in the computer and business worlds. Increase your computer skills and find out how much this technology interests you by joining a computer users group or club at your high school or your community. Access the Internet frequently on your own to observe different Web site designs and find out what is being sold and marketed electronically. What sites do you think are best at promoting products and why? Think about things from a customer's point of view. How easy are the sites to access and use? How are the products displayed and accessed? How competitive are the prices for goods or services?

Make it a goal to come up with your own ideas for a product or service to market on the Web, then do some research. How difficult would it be to deliver the product? What type of financing would be involved? Are there other sites already providing this product or service? How could you make your business unique?

Talk to professionals in your community about their work. Set up information interviews with local business owners to find out what is involved in starting and running a traditional business. Your local chamber of commerce or the Small Business Administration may have classes or publications that would help you learn about starting a business. In addition, set up information interviews with computer consultants, Web site designers, or Internet entrepreneurs. How did they get started? What advice do they have? Is there anything they wish they had done differently? Where do they see the future of e-commerce going?

If your school has a future business owners club, join this group to meet others with similar interests. For hands-on business experience, get a part-time or summer job at any type of store in your area. This work will give you the opportunity to deal with customers (who can sometimes be hard to please), work with handling money, and observe how the store promotes its products and services.

EMPLOYERS

Internet entrepreneurs are self-employed, and sometimes they may employ people to work under them. Some Internet entrepreneurs may be hired to begin a business for someone else.

STARTING OUT

Professionals in the field advise those just starting out to work for someone else to gain experience in the business world before beginning their own business. The Internet is a good resource to use to find employment. There are many sites that post job openings. Local employment agencies and newspapers and trade magazines also list job opportunities. In addition, your college career services office should be able to provide you with help locating a job. Networking with college alumni and people in your computer users groups may also provide job leads.

ADVANCEMENT

Advancement opportunities depend on the business, its success, and the individual's goals. Internet entrepreneurs who are successful may enter other business fields or consulting. Or they may advance to higher level management positions or other larger Internet-based businesses. Some entrepreneurs establish a business and then sell it only to begin another business venture. The Internet world is constantly changing because of technological advancements. This state of flux means that a wide variety of possibilities are available to those working in the field. "There is no solid career path in the Internet field," says Dave Wright. "Your next career may not even be developed yet."

EARNINGS

Income for Internet entrepreneurs is usually tied to the profitability of the business. Entrepreneurs are self-employed and their income will depend on the success of the business. Those just starting out may actually have no earnings, while those with a business that has been existence for several years may have annual earnings between $25,000 and $50,000. Some in the field may earn much more than this amount. John Axne estimates that those who have good technical skills and can do such things as create the database program for a Web site may have higher salaries, in the $60,000 to $125,000 range.

Entrepreneurs are almost always responsible for their own medical, disability, and life insurances. Retirement plans must also be self-funded and self-directed.

WORK ENVIRONMENT

Internet entrepreneurs may work out of a home or private office. Some Internet entrepreneurs may be required to work on-site at a corporation or small business.

The entrepreneur must deal with the stresses of starting a business, keeping it going, dealing with deadlines and customers, and coping with problems as they arise. They must also work long hours to develop and manage their business venture; many entrepreneurs work more than 40 hours a week. Evening or weekend work may also be required.

In addition, these professionals must spend time researching, reading, and checking out the competition to keep informed about the latest technology and business trends. Their intensive computer work can result in eyestrain, hand and wrist injuries, and back pain.

OUTLOOK

Online commerce is a very new and exciting field with tremendous potential, and it is likely that growth will continue over the long term. However, it is important to keep in mind that the failure rate for new businesses, even traditional ones, is fairly high. Some experts predict that in the next few years, 80 to 90 percent of dot-coms will either close or be acquired by other companies. The survivors will be small businesses that are able to find niche markets, anticipate trends, adapt to market and technology changes, and plan for a large enough financial margin to turn a profit. Analysts also anticipate that the amount of business-to-business e-commerce will surpass business-to-consumer sales.

Internet entrepreneurs with the most thorough education and experience and who have done their research will have the best opportunities for success. For those who are adventurous and interested in using new avenues for selling products and services, the Internet offers many possibilities.

FOR MORE INFORMATION

To learn more about the information technology industry and e-commerce, contact

Information Technology Association of America
1401 Wilson Boulevard, Suite 1100
Arlington, VA 22209-2318
Tel: 703-522-5055
http://www.itaa.org

For certification information, contact

Institute for Certification of Computing Professionals
2350 East Devon Avenue, Suite 115
Des Plaines, IL 60018-4610
Tel: 800-843-8227
Email: office@iccp.org

For information on certification, contact

Institute of Certified Professional Managers
James Madison University
MSC 5504
Harrisonburg, VA 22807-0001
Tel: 800-568-4120

Email: icpmcm@jmu.edu
http://icpm.biz/

The Small Business Administration offers helpful information on starting a business. For information on state offices and additional references, visit its Web site.
Small Business Administration
409 Third Street, SW
Washington, DC 20416-0001
Tel: 800-827-5722
Email: answerdesk@sba.gov
http://www.sba.gov

Check out the following online magazine specializing in topics of interest to entrepreneurs:
entrepreneur.com
http://entrepreneur.com

Lawn and Gardening Service Owners

OVERVIEW

Lawn and gardening service owners maintain the lawns of residential and commercial properties. They cut grass and shrubbery, clean yards, and treat grass with fertilizer and insecticides. They may also landscape, which involves the arrangement of lawns, trees, and bushes. There are about 1.5 million people employed in the grounds maintenance industry. Nearly 25 percent of landscapers, groundskeepers, and nursery workers are self-employed.

HISTORY

If you've ever visited or seen photographs of the Taj Mahal in India or Versailles in France, then you've seen some elaborate examples of the lawns and gardens of the world. For as long as people have built grand palaces, they have designed lawns and gardens to surround them. Private, irrigated gardens of ancient Egypt and Persia were regarded as paradise with their thick, green vegetation and cool shade. In the 16th century, Italians kept gardens that wound about fountains, columns, and steps. The English developed the "cottage-style" gardens to adhere to the natural surroundings. Early American gardens, such as those surrounding Monticello in Virginia, were inspired by this English style.

The English also inspired the Georgian style of house design in the 18th century that caught on across Europe and America. Rows of houses down city blocks were designed as units, their yards hidden behind the houses and away from the streets. Lawn care as a business blossomed with the growth of population and home ownership between the Civil War and World War I. The sport of golf also became popular among the rich at this time, spurring further development of lawn care products and machinery. Since World War II, many people now hire lawn maintenance professionals to keep up and improve the look of their personal lawns and gardens.

THE JOB

Lawn and gardening businesses may choose to offer only a few services, such as lawn mowing and hedge clipping. But some businesses offer a large number of services, from simple cleaning to the actual design of the yard. Some lawn services specialize in organic lawn care. They rely on natural fertilizers and applications to control insects and lawn diseases instead of applying toxic chemicals to treat lawns.

When working for private homeowners, lawn and gardening services do yard work once or twice a week for each client. They arrive at the residence with equipment, such as a push or riding mower, an aerator, and a blower vac. Workers cut the grass and "weed-eat," trimming the weeds at the edges of the houses and fences. They also apply fertilizer and insecticide to the lawn to keep the grass healthy and use an aerator to run over the yard to make holes in the topsoil and allow more airflow.

Lawn and gardening service owners participate in all aspects of the business, including the labor. They plant grass seed in areas where there is little growth, and use blowers to blow leaves and other debris from the yard, sidewalks, and driveway. Lawn services are often called in after storms and other natural disasters to clean up and repair lawns.

"There are a lot of little services you can throw in to keep you busy," says Sam Morgan, who operates a lawn care service in Dallas, Texas. He does general lawn maintenance for residential yards and some rental properties. "Having some rental property can be good," he says. "It's year-round work. But it can also be dirty work; you have to pick up a lot of trash."

In addition to mowing yards and weed-eating, he assists with planting flower beds, cleaning house gutters, and some light tree work. Tree care involves the pruning and trimming of branches. Lawn and gardening services may need to remove dead or unwanted trees before planting new ones. They may also offer landscaping services, offering advice on arranging the lawn. Service owners assist in positioning trees, bushes, fountains, flower beds, and lighting. They may also put up wood or metal fencing, and install sprinkler systems.

"I started the business on a shoestring," Morgan says. "But I learned early that you have to have good equipment." He now owns a commercial mower that can handle 200 yards a week.

Lawn and gardening service owners have other responsibilities than just lawn and garden care. As owners, they are responsible for the business end of the service. To stay in business, owners must balance the budget, collect on accounts, repair or replace equipment when necessary, order supplies, and, depending on the size of the business, may hire and manage other employees.

In addition to working on the demanding yard work, Morgan spends much of his time attending to business details, such as keeping tax records, making phone calls, and preparing estimates and bills.

REQUIREMENTS

High School

Take agriculture, shop, and other courses that will help you gain familiarity with the machinery, fertilizers, and chemicals used in lawn maintenance. Agriculture courses will also teach you about different grasses and plants, and how to care for them. Joining associations such as the National FFA Organization (formerly the Future Farmers of America) and 4-H can give you additional experience with horticulture. Business and accounting courses are also useful to learn about record keeping, budgeting, and finances.

Postsecondary Training

After high school, you can learn about lawn maintenance on the job, either by assisting someone with an established lawn care business, or by taking on a few residential customers yourself. Though a college degree is not necessary, lawn and gardening service owners benefit from advanced courses such as small business management and finance to help run their business.

Certification or Licensing

Certification is not required, but many lawn and garden service owners choose to earn professional certifications from the Professional Landcare Network. The network offers the following certification designations: certified landscape professional, certified landscape technician-interior, certified landscape technician-exterior, certified turfgrass professional, certified turfgrass professional-cool season lawns, and certified ornamental landscape professional. Depending on the certification, applicants must pass a multiple-choice examination or a hands-on field test.

Most states require lawn care professionals who apply pesticides to be licensed. This usually involves passing a written examination on the safe use and disposal of toxic chemicals.

Other Requirements

As entrepreneurs, lawn and gardening service owners need to have people skills and be self-motivated to successfully promote their own business and attract clients.

"I'm a good salesman," Sam Morgan says. He also emphasizes the need to be committed to doing a quality job for every customer. Service owners should have an eye for detail to notice all the areas where lawns need work. They must also be in fairly good health to withstand the hard labor that the job calls for, often during the heat of the summer.

EXPLORING

If you've made some extra money mowing lawns for your neighbors, then you're already familiar with many of the aspects of a lawn care service. Walking behind a power mower during the hottest days of the year may make you miserable, but early experience in keeping your next-door neighbor's lawn looking nice is a great opportunity for self-employment. Other sources for potential clients are private homeowners, apartment complex communities, golf courses, and parks. Look into volunteer and part-time work with botanical gardens, greenhouses, and park and recreation crews.

Opportunities to learn how to care for a lawn and garden are no further than your own backyard. Experiment with planting and maintaining different varieties of flowers, shrubs, or trees. Chances are, you'll gain valuable experience and your parents will thank you!

In addition to getting dirt under your fingernails, you can also explore the lawn and garden services by reading magazines and books on lawn and garden care. Cable television stations, such as Home and Garden Television (HGTV), feature programming about gardening.

Every summer, many high school students find reliable work mowing lawns. But many of these students tire of the work early in the summer. Be persistent in seeking out work all summer long. You should also be committed to doing good work. You'll have stiff competition from professional lawn care businesses that offer more services, own commercial machinery, and have extensive knowledge of fertilizers and pesticides. Some lawn care companies also hire students for summer work.

EMPLOYERS

Lawn and gardening service owners work primarily for private homeowners, though they may also contract work with commercial properties. Condos, hotels, apartment complexes, golf courses, sports fields, and parks all require regular lawn service.

Owners who choose to build their own business face challenges such as covering the costs of start-up and establishing a client base. To defray these costs and risks, many choose to purchase and operate an existing business. There are a number of franchise opportunities in lawn care that, for a fee, will assist you in promoting your business and building a clientele. Emerald Green Lawn Care, Liqui-Green Lawn Care, and Lawn Doctor are just a few. NaturaLawn of America is a franchise that provides organic-based lawn care.

STARTING OUT

Most lawn and gardening service owners start out working for established services and work their way into positions of management or higher responsibility. A typical entry-level job is that of the landscape service technician. After a few years on the job, promising technicians may be promoted to supervisor positions such as regional or branch managers. According to the Professional Landcare Network, "Once a supervisory position is reached, leadership is the key to success." Workers who are organized, show strong leadership, and can make decisions quickly and wisely will have the best chances for promotion and may choose to start up their own business.

However, not all service owners follow this route. Sam Morgan's lawn service was not his first venture into entrepreneurship; he had once owned a number of dry cleaners. After selling the dry cleaners, he went to work for a chemical company. When the company downsized, Morgan was faced with finding a new job. He decided to turn to lawn care.

"I just went to Sears and bought a mower," he says. Since then, he's been able to invest in commercial machinery that can better handle the demands of the work, and he's found a number of ways to increase business. "I bill once a month," he says. "I get more business that way." He's also expanding his service to include some light landscaping, such as shrub work and planting small trees.

Depending on the business, start-up costs can vary. To purchase commercial quality equipment, the initial investment can be between $3,000 and $4,000. To buy into a franchise, however, will cost thousands of dollars more.

ADVANCEMENT

Once lawn and gardening service owners establish their own businesses, advancement can come in the form of expanded services. Some lawn professionals offer equipment and supply sales. With extended services, owners can reach out to a larger body of clients, securing larger contracts with golf courses, cities and local communities, and sports teams.

Sam Morgan currently has one employee, but he hopes for his business to grow more, allowing him to hire others. "I don't want to be doing so much of the physical work," he says.

With additional education, owners can also advance into other areas of lawn care and become contractors or landscape architects.

EARNINGS

Earnings in lawn care depend on a number of factors, such as geographic location, the size of the business, and the level of experience. Lawn care services generally make more money in areas of the country that have mild winters, offering more months of lawn growth and, as a result, requiring more care. The size of the client base also greatly affects earnings. A lawn care professional with a small clientele may make less than $20,000 a year, while the owner of a franchise lawn care company with a number of contracts and a large staff can make more than $100,000.

According to 2007 data from the U.S. Department of Labor, first-line supervisors/managers of landscaping, lawn service, and groundskeeping workers made an average of $18.62 an hour (or $38,720 annually). Salaries ranged from less than $25,270 to $63,280 or more annually. The Professional Landcare Network offers the following summary of earnings potential for management positions: first-level supervisors, $35,000; branch managers, $50,000 or more; regional managers, $60,000s; and successful owners, $100,000 or more.

Since lawn and gardening service owners run their own businesses, they generally do not receive paid sick days or holidays. In addition, they are typically responsible for providing their own insurance and retirement plans.

WORK ENVIRONMENT

To many, working on a lawn or garden is relaxing, and the opportunity to work outdoors during pleasant days of spring and summer is enjoyable. However, the work can also be exhausting and strenuous. Lawn and gardening service owners fully involved in the labor of the business may have to lift heavy equipment from trucks, climb trees, and do a lot of walking, kneeling, and bending on the job. Depending on the nature of the business, service owners may have to exercise caution when handling harmful chemicals used in pesticides. In addition, they have to deal with a loud work environment because machinery such as lawn mowers, weed eaters, and blow vacs can be very noisy.

One benefit of owning a business is the ability to create a flexible work schedule. "Most likely," Sam Morgan says, "during the spring and summer, you can make plenty of money. There's plenty of work to be done." But some of that work may be in the hottest days of the summer, or on rainy days. With your own service, you can arrange to work regular weekday hours, or you can schedule weekends.

OUTLOOK

The benefits of a nice lawn aren't just aesthetic; a well-kept lawn can increase property value and provide a safe place for children to play. According to the National Gardening Association, more than 34 million U.S. households spent $44.7 billion on professional lawn and landscape services in 2006.

This spending promises a good future for lawn care services. The sale of lawn care products is expected to grow as more houses are built and more people recognize the importance of quality lawn care. The Environmental Protection Agency promotes the environmental benefits of a healthy lawn, emphasizing that healthy grass is not only attractive, but controls dust and pollens, provides oxygen, and improves the quality of groundwater. More people now recognize that a nice lawn can increase home value by as much as 20 percent, according to studies.

Technological developments will also aid the industry. With better, more economical equipment, lawn care professionals can do more specialized work in less time, allowing them to keep their service fees low.

FOR MORE INFORMATION

For general information about franchising, specific franchise opportunities, and Introduction to Franchising, *contact the IFA.*

International Franchise Association (IFA)
1501 K Street, NW, Suite 350
Washington, DC 20005-1412
Tel: 202-628-8000
Email: ifa@franchise.org
http://www.franchise.org

To *further explore the agriculture industry and for information on student chapters, contact*
National FFA Organization
6060 FFA Drive
PO Box 68960
Indianapolis, IN 46268-0960
Tel: 317-802-6060
http://www.ffa.org

For *information on certification, careers, internships, and student membership, contact*
Professional Landcare Network
950 Herndon Parkway, Suite 450
Herndon, VA 20170-5528
Tel: 800-395-2522
http://www.landcarenetwork.org/cms/home.html

Medical Billing Service Owners

OVERVIEW

Medical billers help doctors and other health care professionals receive payment for services. They send bills to patients, private insurance companies, Medicare, and other insurers. Using special software, they file insurance claims electronically via an Internet connection. They keep files on patients and insurers, and use medical codes when filing claims. Most billers work from their home offices, though some work in the offices of doctors and clinics. Medical billers are sometimes known as *electronic billing professionals, claims processing professionals,* and *medical provider consultants.*

HISTORY

Group health insurance plans first developed in the 1940s as a result of the growing expense of medical care. Since then, doctors have received much of their payment from insurance companies, rather than individual patients. With more patients using these "third-party" payers, doctors began to need assistance in dealing with the extra work of completing and submitting insurance forms. Medical billing services developed in response to this demand.

Accountants, administrative assistants, and people working at home took on the bookkeeping responsibilities of doctors' offices. When personal computers came into common use in the 1980s, medical billing changed from paper-based claims to electronic claims. Filing claims electronically required modems and specially designed software, and medical billing services were in even greater demand;

doctors didn't have the time to learn the complexities of submitting electronic claims. Demand for outside billing services increased even more after 1990, when the federal government ruled that doctors, and not elderly patients, were responsible for submitting claims to Medicare.

THE JOB

No matter how many injuries or illnesses you may have had in high school, you probably have not had much experience with insurance companies. Your parents, however, have certainly dealt with the responsibilities of maintaining insurance coverage for the family. They've saved bills, submitted claims, and dealt with doctors' offices and insurance agencies. Health care coverage is considered an important and necessary benefit of full-time employment, so much so that many people make job decisions based on the quality of insurance available. Insurance has become a major concern as people struggle to meet the rising costs of health care.

So you can imagine the difficulties facing doctors in billing patients, filing claims, and keeping accurate patient accounts. In addition to private insurance companies, doctors receive payment from Medicare (a government insurance program for people over the age of 65 and for people with disabilities), Medicaid (a government insurance program for people of all ages within certain income limits), and workers' compensation (insurance from employers to cover employees injured on the job). To get paid by these insurers, doctors must submit detailed claims. These claims include information about diagnosis and treatment, and require a knowledge of medical codes.

Medical billers handle the filing of these claims. They work out of their homes or offices, and take on as many clients as they choose. According to Merl Coslick, the executive director of the Electronic Medical Billing Network of America, a national trade association, the majority of medical billers have three or fewer clients. Medical billing is often seen as supplementary income, and more than three clients may require a staff and much more time. Felicitas Cortez is one of these billers keeping her service small to allow her to work from her home office and spend time with her children. Her father is a physician, and part of his practice involves managing a nursing home. Cortez handles the billing for the nursing home patients. Most of the patients are on Medicare. Cortez designed a form that the doctor takes when visiting patients. On each patient's form, the doctor lists what services the patient requires, along with his diagnosis. Once a month, these forms are sent to Cortez, who maintains records for the patients. "The record includes insurance information, such as the Medicare number, whether the patient is on public aid, and if there's any secondary insurance," Cortez says.

Cortez must also convert the doctor's diagnosis to a special medical code. Medical billers use ICD codes that represent diagnoses, and CPT codes that represent treatment procedures. These codes are standard for private insurers across the country, and for Medicare. "I have a book to consult for the codes," Cortez says, "but it can get complicated. I don't have a medical background, and there are so many kinds of pneumonia, for example. There are about 100 codes for pneumonia, and insurers are very particular." Once she has the codes she needs, Cortez can file a claim. A few insurers still accept claims submitted on paper, but most require electronic filing. Medicare and Medicaid now only accept claims electronically. Electronic claims have proven cheaper than paper billing, and they speed up processing by several weeks. Cortez uses a software system called Medical Office Management Systems, designed specifically for medical billing. After getting online, Cortez lists the physician's National Provider Identifier Standard number (used to identify the physician when billing Medicare, Medicaid, or other insurance), place of service, the International Classification of Diseases code (used when billing for services), the Current Procedural Terminology code (used when billing for services), and the cost of the visit, and electronically submits this claim to a clearinghouse. A clearinghouse is a service that routes the claims to both the primary and secondary insurers. Cortez does this once a week, and reconciles accounts once a month. Payment goes directly from the insurer to the doctor, so Cortez must check with the doctor's office to keep track of paid claims.

Medical billing doesn't just involve computers. There are many phone calls to insurers and doctors to make sure that claims are paid. Cortez must also speak to family members of the nursing home patients to determine how deductibles are to be met.

Some medical billers handle only insurance claims, while others offer many services. They may also send bills to individual patients. They may deal with insurance companies for clients, following up on claims. Medical billers also have to maintain their own financial records, such as business expenses for tax purposes, and payment received from doctors.

REQUIREMENTS
High School
Since medical billers use computers, online services, and special software, classes in computer fundamentals and computer programming are important. Communication and English courses will help

you develop phone skills. Accounting, math, and business management classes will teach you how to keep accurate financial records. Although a medical background isn't necessary, some familiarity with health issues and the health care industry will help you to understand insurance, doctors' offices, and treatments. Take a course in health to gain this familiarity. A business club will allow you to meet local small business owners, and teach you about some of the demands of home-based business ownership.

Postsecondary Training

Medical billers come from a variety of different educational and professional backgrounds. A college education will assist you in soliciting clients, and in performing the billing duties, but it isn't required. Some background in medicine and health care can be helpful to you, but a degree in business management, or in English, can be equally beneficial. You can also benefit from office experience, and an understanding of administrative procedures. Some community colleges offer medical claims billing classes; conferences and workshops in medical billing are also offered by Medicare, private insurers, and clearinghouses.

The billing software you choose for your business may include special training. The Electronic Medical Billing Network of America (EMBN) offers training courses in the New York/New Jersey/Connecticut area, and also distributes computer-based training packages nationwide. Courses include instruction in setting up a medical billing service, billing center management procedures, and claim billing procedures.

Certification or Licensing

Certification isn't required, but it is available from the EMBN upon completion of its training courses. After successfully completing the EMBN training course and passing an examination, medical billing professionals can use the designation, certified electronic medical biller. Other associations, clearinghouses, and software companies also offer certification training courses. Many medical billing professionals work without any kind of certification or licensing at all, but certification can help you in promoting your business to clients.

Other Requirements

Medical billers need the patience for filling out long, detailed forms, transforming treatments and diagnoses to codes, and maintaining client records. You should be organized, and have an understanding of spreadsheet and word processing programs and online services. Obviously, a head for figures is important, but people skills are also very valuable. Felicitas Cortez must deal sensitively with the nursing home patients and their families in discussing payments and insurance deductibles, but must be firm and persistent when dealing with insurance companies. "You have to speak to a lot of different people in different ways to get what you need," she says. You also have to keep up on laws affecting insurers, doctors, and billing methods.

EXPLORING

Many volunteer opportunities in the health care industry are available to high school students. Assisting at a hospital or nursing home will give you some background in medical terminology and a doctor's routine. Working part-time for a pharmacist can give you similar experience, and may include working with Medicare and Medicaid forms, and preparing medications for nursing homes. Many school clubs elect treasurers who handle receipts, payments, and bills; either volunteer for the position, or assist the adviser in charge of money matters. A part-time administrative position with a local insurance agency, or any area business, can give you valuable experience in handling calls, preparing forms, and completing billing procedures.

EMPLOYERS

From chiropractors to psychiatrists, health care professionals must deal with insurers, billing patients, and keeping accurate payment records. Anybody who needs to file claims with third-party payers, including personal trainers and physical therapists, can benefit from the services of a medical billing professional. Medical billing service owners may work with one specific area of health care, or they may have a diverse clientele. Their clients may be in their local area, or they may work with clients in other cities, contacting them by phone, fax, and email.

STARTING OUT

Try to get some experience with medical billing before investing in the business. Working in a doctor's office can quickly familiarize you with the job's requirements, and will give you experience that you can promote to potential clients. Be very sure that the business is for you, because start-up costs can run into thousands of dollars for computer and printer, database and marketing software, and medical billing software. Be very careful about what billing software you select; there are many different programs available. The cost of software ranges from $100 to $12,000. In general, the software used by active billers around the country costs between $500 and $1,000.

The lower cost programs may offer all you need for a small business. However, more expensive programs may also include additional services, such as access to a clearinghouse that routes your electronic claims to primary and secondary insurers.

Make sure you can take on enough clients to support your business. Most general care physicians have their own billing staffs. You will have to convince these doctors that they will benefit from contracting an outside billing service, and that you have the skills to handle the billing and improve payment methods. By joining a professional association, you can receive guidance and support from other medical billers.

ADVANCEMENT

The majority of people with their own billing services prefer to keep their businesses small, handling only a few clients. But it is possible to expand your business into a service for several doctors. According to Merl Coslick of the EMBN, there are about 600 companies grossing more than $1 million a year and processing tens of thousands of claims a week. Obviously, it takes a much greater investment to expand—medical billing service owners will need a staff, additional office equipment, and commercial office space.

Service owners can still advance into other areas while maintaining a small operation. Some experienced billing professionals serve as consultants for doctors' offices. They train an office's internal billing staff, help build billing records, and oversee the electronic claims filing.

EARNINGS

Some medical billers charge their clients for each claim processed; others charge a percentage of the insurance payment. Some billers have contracts with doctors and charge flat weekly or monthly fees. No salary surveys have yet been conducted on independent billing service owners, but Coslick estimates that a service processing 300 claims per month can make $10,000 per year for each client. Though most owners of medical billing services choose to operate only part time, those working full time may be able to process 1,500 claims or more per month.

Since they are self-employed, medical billing service owners do not receive paid sick days or holidays and are responsible for providing their own insurance and retirement plans.

WORK ENVIRONMENT

Most medical billers work in the comfort of their own home offices. Although they don't have any direct supervision, clients regularly contact them to check on the status of an insurance payment. They spend much of their time on the phone and on the computer. In some cases, billers may visit a client's office to collect forms; some billers, however, simply use fax machines and messenger services to exchange information. Billers who offer consulting services spend some time in doctors' offices working closely with billing staff members. The hours per week will depend on the number of clients. Serving only a few clients requires approximately 20 hours a week; any more than three clients requires 40 hours or more a week. It is not necessary to keep regular business hours, since so much work is done at the computer using electronic systems. Medical billers can set their own schedules, working evenings and weekends if they prefer.

OUTLOOK

Although many Americans are still without health insurance, some government programs are actively involved in providing insurance to the elderly, children, people with disabilities, and those with low incomes. The Centers for Medicare and Medicaid Services (CMS), which administers Medicare, Medicaid, and the State Children's Health Insurance Program provides health insurance for approximately 101.2 million Americans. This number will increase as the baby-boomer generation grows older, and as the Children's Health Insurance Program evolves. A CMS study projected health care expenditures to reach $4.2 trillion by 2017. This will mean the filing of billions of insurance claims. Doctors will require even more assistance in billing, and receiving payments, particularly as more billing procedures are done electronically. Merl Coslick believes that more billing professionals will become consultants to doctors' offices. Within three to five years, he predicts, the bulk of billing will be done internally, and consultants will be needed to train staff in medical billing software.

FOR MORE INFORMATION

For information about government insurance programs and health care statistics, contact
Centers for Medicare & Medicaid Services
7500 Security Boulevard

Baltimore, MD 21244-1850
Tel: 877-267-2323
http://www.cms.hhs.gov

To *learn more about the career of medical biller and certification, subscribe to a monthly newsletter, and to learn about training and publications, contact*
Electronic Medical Billing Network of America
51 Eton Court
Bedminster, NJ 07921-1605
Tel: 908-470-4100
Email: merl@medicalbillingnetwork.com
http://www.medicalbillingnetwork.com

INTERVIEW

Felicitas Cortez owns a medical billing service in Orland Park, Illinois. She discussed her career with the editors of Careers in Focus: Entrepreneurs.

Q. How long have you worked in the field?
A. I started my medical billing business almost 10 years ago. I am responsible for all billing services related to my father's medical practice.

Q. What are some of the pros and cons of your job?
A. Flexibility is the biggest pro of this job. I am able to work from home, and keep hours convenient to my schedule. Since my billing program is online, I am able to work during the day or night. Services are billed monthly, so while I have to send my transmittals in a timely manner, there is no mad rush or weekly deadline.

There is less paperwork now that most insurance carriers insist on computerized submissions. However, there is still a lot of data entry to be done, especially with new patients—this can be tedious. Also, it's important to stay informed of any changes in procedures, diagnosis codes, or information regarding the patients' insurance coverage.

Q. What are the most important personal and professional qualities for medical billers?
A. You'll need patience. It's a slow process to build your data file, become familiar with a new program or changing diagnosis codes, or even to keep up with new insurance or Medicare regulations.

Sometimes you may have to reach a patient or their family to get additional information, or perhaps inquire with insurance headquarters or Medicare to find out why a claim was rejected. Even when it's difficult to get a straight answer or when you are passed from one department to another, it's important to maintain a professional voice and attitude. After all, you are acting as a representative of the doctor's office or the hospital's billing department.

Q. What advice would you give to young people who are interested in the field?

A. The computer is going to be your most important piece of equipment. It will be used to store data as well as send and receive insurance claims—so it's important to be comfortable working with computers.

Q. What is the future employment outlook for medical billers?

A. I think medical billers will be in great demand. As more and more insurance carriers move toward paperless claims, doctors and hospitals will rely on medical billers to process and reconcile their billing needs. Medical billing services can also be used by all medical professionals including physicians, dentists, physical therapists, and nurse practitioners.

Personal Chefs

QUICK FACTS

School Subjects
Family and consumer science
Health

Personal Skills
Communication/ideas
Leadership/management

Work Environment
Primarily indoors
Primarily multiple locations

Minimum Education Level
Some postsecondary training

Salary Range
$35,000 to $42,500 to
$50,000

Certification or Licensing
Voluntary

Outlook
Faster than the average

DOT
313

GOE
N/A

NOC
N/A

O*NET-SOC
35-1011.00

OVERVIEW

Personal chefs prepare menus for individuals and their families, purchase the ingredients for the meals, then cook, package, and store the meals in the clients' own kitchens. Approximately 9,000 personal chefs work across the United States and Canada, cooking for busy families, seniors, people with disabilities, and others who don't have the time or the ability to prepare meals for themselves.

HISTORY

Since the beginning of time, humans have experimented with food and cooking techniques in efforts to create simpler, quicker, more balanced meals. The development of pottery and agriculture was the earliest step toward better cooking, after years of using skulls and bones as cooking pots and hunting for meat. Cooks have always built from the progress of previous generations; Catherine de Medici of Italy is often credited with introducing, in the 16th century, masterful cooking to the French where fine cuisine developed into an art form.

Though royalty, the famous, and the wealthy have long hired private chefs to work in their kitchens, personal chefs have only recently come onto the scene. Within the last 15 years, experienced cooks, either looking to expand their catering and restaurant businesses, or burned out from working as chefs, have begun meeting the demand for quick, easy meals that taste homemade. Men and women are holding down demanding, time-consuming jobs, and looking for alternatives to microwave dinners, fast food, and frozen pizzas. David MacKay founded the first professional association for personal chefs, the

United States Personal Chef Association (USPCA), in 1991, and helps to establish more than 400 new businesses every year. The American Personal & Private Chef Association (APPCA), founded by Candy Wallace, has also developed in recent years, offering training materials and certification to experienced cooks wanting to set up their own businesses.

THE JOB

What will you be cooking for dinner tonight? Spice-rubbed lamb chops with roasted tomatoes? Tarragon chicken with West Indian pumpkin soup? Or maybe turkey parmesan on a bed of red-pepper linguini? If you're rolling up your sleeves and ready to take on a variety of cooking challenges, then a personal chef service may be in your future. People without the time to cook, or without the ability, or those who just plain don't care to cook, are calling upon the services of chefs who will come into their kitchens, throw together delicious meals, then stack the meals in their freezers. A complete meal prepared according to the client's specifications is then only a few minutes of reheating away.

A personal chef is usually someone with a great deal of cooking experience who, for a per-meal fee, will prepare enough meals to last a few days, or a few weeks, for individuals and their families. Personal chefs first meet with a new client to discuss special dietary needs and food preferences. Some clients require vegetarian and low-fat cooking; others have diabetes, or swallowing disorders that require special consideration. (If a personal chef has to do a great deal of research into a special diet plan, they might charge an additional consultation fee.) From these specifications, personal chefs prepare a menu. On the day that they'll be cooking the meals, they visit the grocery store to purchase fresh meats, fish, fruits, and vegetables. At the home of their client, they prepare the meals, package them, label them, and put them in the freezer. Depending on the number of meals, personal chefs spend anywhere from three to eight hours in their client's kitchen. Once they are done, they clean and move onto their next client. Personal chefs are able to control their work hours by limiting the number of clients they take on. They need between five and 10 regular clients to earn a full-time wage.

Most personal chefs prepare the meals in the kitchens of the clients, thereby avoiding the requirements of licensing their own kitchens for commercial use. Greg Porter, a personal chef in South Carolina, is an exception to this norm. As the owner of Masterchef Catering, he is able to prepare meals for his clients in his own commercial kitchen.

A personal chef displays meals she has recently prepared for one of her clients. *(Nati Harnik, AP Photo)*

He had been catering for four years when he began reading articles about personal cheffing. "I researched it on the Internet," he says, "and realized that I was already set up to do it."

Porter pursued training from the APPCA and branched out into the business of personal chef. An article about him in an area newspaper resulted in five new clients. "I don't know of anyone else doing this in South Carolina," Porter says. He prepares upscale, gourmet meals for his clients. "Salmon," he lists, "fresh steak, duck breast, rack of lamb, baby back ribs."

But cooking isn't the only talent called upon for success in the personal chef business. They must also know meals and ingredients that can be easily frozen and reheated without hurting taste and appearance. They should have an understanding of nutrition, health, and sanitation. Good business sense is also important, as personal chefs need to keep financial records, market their service, and schedule and bill clients. They also need to test recipes, experiment with equipment, and look for the most cost-effective ways to purchase groceries. "APPCA doesn't teach you how to cook," Porter says. "It shows you the ins and outs of the business."

Candy Wallace, the founder of APPCA, developed the training course based on her own experiences as owner of "The Serving Spoon," a personal chef service. "The course is about personalizing service," she says, "as well as personalizing business to support your own well-being." Wallace has been in the business for more than 10 years. "I started by taking care of the little old ladies in my neighborhood," she says, referring to how she would drive elderly neighbors to their doctors appointments, run errands for them, and help them prepare meals. She realized she could expand these services. She knew many people longing for the quality and nutrition of a home-cooked meal, but with the ease and speed of the less-healthy, chemical-laden frozen dinners. "I decided to design a program," she says, "for busy corporate women who didn't want their children to glow in the dark."

Most personal chefs try to confine their services to their local areas, or neighborhoods, to keep travel from kitchen to kitchen at a minimum. Sometimes, a good personal chef's services become so valuable to a client, the chef will be invited along on a family's vacation. "I've gone with clients to Palm Springs, Tahoe, Maui," Wallace says.

REQUIREMENTS

High School

A home economics course can give you a good taste of what it's like to be a personal chef. You'll learn something about cooking, budgeting for groceries, and how to use various cooking equipment and appliances. A course in health will teach you about nutrition and a proper diet. Take a business course that offers lessons in bookkeeping and accounting to help you prepare for the record-keeping aspect of the job. A composition or communications course can help you develop the writing skills you'll need for self-promotion. Join a business organization for the chance to meet with small business owners, and to learn about the fundamentals of business operation.

Postsecondary Training
Both the APPCA and the USPCA offer self-study courses and semi-nars on the personal chef business. These courses are not designed to teach people how to cook, but rather how to start a service, how to market it, how much to charge for services, and other concerns specific to the personal chef business. These courses also offer reci-pes for foods that freeze and store well.

A formal education isn't required of personal chefs, but a good culinary school can give you valuable cooking experience. "You must be well trained," Greg Porter advises. Porter holds an associ-ate's degree in the culinary arts from the Johnson and Wales Uni-versity, which has one of the highest-ranked cooking schools in the country. With a degree, you can pursue work in restaurants, hotels, health care facilities, and other industries needing the expertise of professional cooks. Culinary programs include courses in vegetar-ian cooking, menu design, food safety and sanitation, along with courses like economics and math. "But what will teach you more," Porter says, "is working part-time for a restaurant, or a caterer, to learn the business. I've sold food, catered, managed, owned a restau-rant—I've done it all, to learn the whole business inside out."

Certification or Licensing
To become a certified personal chef with the USPCA, you must work for at least two years as a personal chef. You're required to complete written and practical exams and meet educational requirements. The APPCA, in conjunction with the American Culinary Federa-tion, offers the personal certified chef designation to applicants who have at least four years of professional cooking experience, at least one year of employment as a personal chef, and who pass written and practical examinations. The APPCA also offers the personal certified executive chef designation to applicants who have at least six years of professional cooking experience, have worked a mini-mum of two years as a personal chef, and pass written and practical examinations. One-quarter to one-half of the personal chefs work-ing in the United States and Canada are certified, but certification isn't required to work in the business.

Because you'll be working in the kitchens of your clients, you won't need licensing, or to adhere to the health department regu-lations of commercial kitchens. A few states, however, do charge permit fees, and require some inspections of the vehicle in which you carry groceries and cooking equipment.

Other Requirements

Porter emphasizes that a person should have an outgoing personality to be successful as a personal chef. "Customer service is the most important thing," he says. "If you're not people oriented, you can just hang it up." A strong work ethic and an ambition to succeed are also very important—you'll be promoting your business, building a client list, and handling administrative details all yourself. You'll need patience, too, not only as you prepare quality meals, but as you wait for your business to develop and your client list to grow. You should be a creative thinker, capable of designing interesting menus within the specifications of the client. And, of course, keep in mind that you'll be cooking several meals a day, every day. So it may not be enough to just "like" cooking; you'll need a passion for it.

EXPLORING

The most valuable exploration you can do is to spend time in the kitchen. Learn how to properly use the cooking appliances and utensils. Experiment with recipes. Various Web posting sites include recipes that are good to freeze and store. This way you'll learn what meals would work best in a personal chef service. Cook for friends and family, and volunteer to work at high school banquets and soup kitchens. Contact the professional associations for names of personal chefs in your area. Some chefs participate in mentoring programs to help people learn about the business. Look into part-time work with a restaurant, cafe, or caterer. Many caterers hire assistants on a temporary basis to help with large events.

EMPLOYERS

Approximately 9,000 personal chefs are employed in the United States and Canada. Nearly all personal chef services are owned and operated by individuals, though some well-established chefs serving a largely populated, affluent area may hire assistants. Aspiring personal chefs who live in one of these areas and have some cooking experience and education may be able to hire on as a cook with a big personal chef operation. But most personal chefs will be in business for themselves and will promote their services in areas near their home.

The majority of people who use the services of personal chefs are working couples who have household incomes over $70,000. Most of these couples have children. Personal chefs also work for people with disabilities and senior citizens. "A lot of clients are seniors," Candy Wallace of the APPCA says. "They want to stay in their own homes, but never want to see the inside of a grocery store or a kitchen again. Some of these clients are in their 90s."

STARTING OUT

David MacKay, founder of USPCA, emphasizes that the career of personal chef is really for those who have tried other careers and have some experience in the food and service industry. The personal chef courses being offered by USPCA-accredited community colleges may eventually change this and may attract people with little cooking experience into the business. For now, though, a personal chef course and seminar isn't really enough to get you started unless you also have a culinary education, or a great deal of knowledge about cooking.

If you feel confident that you have the cooking knowledge necessary to prepare good-tasting, well-balanced meals for paying customers, then you should consider training through either the APPCA or the USPCA. Once you have a good sense of the requirements and demands of the job, you can start seeking out clients. Because you'll be cooking with the stoves and appliances of your clients, you don't need to invest much money into starting up your business. An initial investment of about $1,000 will buy you some quality cookware and utensils. But you'll also need a reliable vehicle, as you'll be driving to the grocery store and to the homes of your clients every day.

Volunteer your services for a week or two to friends and neighbors who you think might be interested in hiring you. Print up some fliers and cards, and post your name on community bulletin boards. You may have to offer a low, introductory price to entice clients to try your services.

ADVANCEMENT

Most personal chefs only cook for one or two clients daily, so maintaining between five and 10 clients will keep them pretty busy. If a personal chef is able to attract many more customers than they can handle, it may be beneficial for them to hire assistants and to raise their prices. As they grow their business, personal chefs may choose to expand into other areas, like catering large events, writing food-related articles for a local newspaper or magazine, or teaching cooking classes. They may also meet with owners of grocery stores and restaurants, consulting with them about developing their own meal take-out services.

EARNINGS

According to the USPCA, salaries for personal chefs range from about $35,000 annually on the low end to $50,000 on the high end.

Some chefs with assistant cooks and a number of clients can make much more than that, but businesses composed of a single owner/ operator average about $40,000 per year.

Personal chefs usually sell their services as a package deal—typically $250 to $300 for 10 meals for two people, with a fee of $10 to $15 for each additional meal. A complete package may take a full day to prepare. This may seem like a very good wage, but it's important to remember that personal chefs must pay for the groceries. Though they will be able to save some money by buying staples in bulk, and by planning their menus efficiently, they'll also be spending a lot on fresh meat, fish, and vegetables. One-third or less of a personal chef's 10-meal package fee will go toward the expense of its ingredients.

Since personal chefs operate their own businesses, they generally do not receive paid sick days or holidays. In addition, they are typically responsible for providing their own insurance and retirement plans.

WORK ENVIRONMENT

Greg Porter likes the "personal" aspect of working as a personal chef. "My customers become friends," he says. He appreciates being able to prepare meals based on the individual tastes of his customers, rather than "the 300 people coming into a restaurant." Many personal chefs enter the business after burning out on the demands of restaurant work. Many personal chefs enjoy making their own schedule, avoiding the late nights, long hours, and weekends of restaurant service.

Though personal chefs don't work in their own homes, they don't travel that much. They will have to visit a grocery store every morning for fresh meats and produce, but most of the hours of each workday will be spent in one or two kitchens. Freezer space, pantries, and stoves obviously won't be as large as those in a commercial kitchen, but work spaces are generally more inviting and homey than those in the back of a restaurant. Personal chefs work entirely on their own, with little supervision by their clients. In most cases, their clients will be at work, allowing them to create their meals, and their messes, in private.

OUTLOOK

The personal chef industry is growing in leaps and bounds, and will continue to do so. The APPCA reports that industry experts predict that employment in the field will double in the next five to eight years. The career has become recognized by culinary institutes, and some schools are beginning to include personal chef courses as part of their curriculums. The national publications *Entrepreneur, Time,*

US News and World Report, and others have listed personal chef services as one of the hottest new businesses.

Though the basics of the job will likely remain the same in future years, it is subject to some trends. Personal chefs will need to keep up with diet fads and new health concerns, as well as trends in gourmet cooking. As the career gains prominence, states may regulate it more rigorously, requiring certain health inspections and permits. Some states may also begin to require special food safety and sanitation training.

FOR MORE INFORMATION

For information on certification for personal chefs, contact
American Culinary Federation
180 Center Place Way
St. Augustine, FL 32095-8859
Tel: 800-624-9458
Email: acf@acfchefs.net
http://www.acfchefs.org

The APPCA holds seminars, offers certification, and maintains an informative Web site with a personal chef message board.
American Personal & Private Chef Association (APPCA)
4572 Delaware Street
San Diego, CA 92116-1005
Tel: 800-644-8389
Email: info@personalchef.com
http://www.personalchef.com

The USPCA offers training courses, certification, and mentorship.
United States Personal Chef Association (USPCA)
610 Quantum Road, NE
Rio Rancho, NM 87124-4506
Tel: 800-995-2138
http://www.uspca.com

Personal Shoppers

OVERVIEW

People who don't have the time or the ability to go shopping for clothes, gifts, groceries, and other items use the services of *personal shoppers*. Personal shoppers shop department stores, look at catalogs, and surf the Internet for the best buys and most appropriate items for their clients. Relying on a sense of style and an ability to spot a bargain, a personal shopper helps clients develop a wardrobe and find gifts for friends, relatives, and employees. Though personal shoppers work all across the country, their services are in most demand in large, metropolitan areas.

HISTORY

For decades, American retailers have been working to create easier ways to shop. Mail-order was an early innovation. Catalog companies such as Montgomery Wards and Sears, Roebuck and Co. started business in the late 19th century to meet the shopping needs of people living in rural areas and small towns. Many consumers relied on mail-order for everything from suits and dresses to furniture and stoves; Sears even sold automobiles through the mail. Shopping for food, clothes, and gifts was considered a household chore, a responsibility that belonged to women. By the late 1800s, shopping had developed into a popular pastime in metropolitan areas. Wealthy women of leisure turned downtown shopping districts into the busiest sections of their cities, as department stores, boutiques, tea shops, and cafes evolved to serve them.

As more women joined the workforce after World War II, retailers worked to make their shopping areas more convenient. Supermarkets, shopping centers, and malls became popular. Toward the end of the

QUICK FACTS

School Subjects
Business
Family and consumer science

Personal Skills
Following instructions
Helping/teaching

Work Environment
Primarily indoors
Primarily multiple locations

Minimum Education Level
High school diploma

Salary Range
$10,000 to $22,000 to $36,000

Certification or Licensing
None available

Outlook
About as fast as the average

DOT
296

GOE
11.08.01

NOC
N/A

O*NET-SOC
N/A

20th century, shoppers began looking for even more simplicity and convenience. In the 1990s, many companies began to market their products via the Internet. In addition to Internet commerce, overworked men and women are turning to personal shoppers, professional organizers, and personal assistants to fulfill their shopping needs.

THE JOB

Looking for a job where you get to shop all the time, tell people what to wear, and spend somebody else's money? Though this may seem to describe the life of the personal shopper, it's not quite accurate. For one thing, personal shoppers don't get to shop all the time; they will be spending some time in stores and browsing catalogs, but they're often looking for something very specific and working as quickly as they can. And they do not so much tell people what to wear as teach them how to best match outfits, what colors suit them, and what styles are most appropriate for their workplaces. Yes, personal shoppers spend someone else's money, but it's all for someone else's closet. So, if you're not too disillusioned, read on: Working as a personal shopper may still be right for you.

Personal shoppers help people who are unable or uninterested in doing their own shopping. They are hired to look for that perfect gift for a difficult-to-please aunt. They work for senior citizens, or people with disabilities, to do their grocery shopping and run other shopping errands. Personal shoppers help professionals create a nice, complete wardrobe. All the while, they rely on their knowledge of the local marketplace to do the shopping quickly and efficiently.

Some personal shoppers use their backgrounds in other areas to assist clients. Those with a background in cosmetology may work as *image consultants,* advising clients on their hair, clothes, and makeup. Another shopper may have some experience with antiques and will help clients locate particular items. An interior decorator may shop for furniture and art to decorate a home.

Personal shoppers who offer wardrobe consultation will need to visit their client's home and evaluate his or her clothes. They help their clients determine what additional clothes and accessories they'll need, and they offer advice on what jackets to wear with what pants or what skirt to wear with what blouse. Together with their client, personal shoppers determine what additional clothes are needed to complete the wardrobe, and they come up with a budget. Then it's off to the stores.

Irene Kato owns I Kan Do It Personal Shopper, Etc., a personal shopping service. She offers a variety of services, including at-home wardrobe consultation, closet organization, and gift shopping. "Most of my shopping so far has been for clothes," Kato says. "I have a fairly good idea of what I'm looking for so I don't spend too much time in any one store if I don't see what I want right away. I can usually find two or three choices for my client and rarely have to shop another day." Kato spends about two to three hours every other day shopping and about two hours a day in her office working on publicity, her budget, and corresponding with clients. Shopping for one client can take about three hours. "I have always enjoyed shopping," Kato says, "and especially like finding bargains. Waiting in lines, crowds, etc., does not bother me."

Personal shoppers often cater to professionals needing business attire and wardrobe consultation. A smaller part of their business will be shopping for gifts. They may even supplement their business by running other errands, such as purchasing theater tickets, making deliveries, and going to the post office. Many personal shoppers also work as *professional organizers:* They go into homes and offices to organize desks, kitchens, and closets.

In addition to the actual shopping, personal shoppers have administrative responsibilities. They must keep business records, make phone calls, and schedule appointments. Since personal shopping is a fairly new endeavor, personal shoppers must be expert at educating the public about their services. "A personal shopper has no commodity to sell," Kato says, "only themselves. So it is twice as hard to attract clients." To publicize her business, Kato maintains a Web site (http://www.ikandoit.net) that lists the services she provides and testimonials from clients. She also belongs to two professional organizations that help her network and develop her business: Executive Women International and Giving Referrals to Other Women.

REQUIREMENTS

High School
Take classes in home economics to develop budget and consumer skills as well as learn about fashion and home design. If the class offers a sewing unit, you'll learn about tailoring, and you can develop an eye for clothing sizes. Math, business, and accounting courses will prepare you for the administrative details of the job. English composition and speech classes will help you develop the communication skills you'll need to promote your business and advise clients about their wardrobes.

Postsecondary Training
Many people working as personal shoppers have had experience in other areas of business. They've worked as managers in corpora-

tions or have worked as salespeople in retail stores. But because of the entrepreneurial nature of the career, you don't need any specific kind of education or training. A small-business course at your local community college, along with classes in design, fashion, and consumer science, can help you develop the skills you'll need for the job. If you're unfamiliar with the computer, you should take some classes to learn desktop publishing programs for creating business cards and other publicity material.

Other Requirements

"I seem to have an empathy for people," Irene Kato says. "After talking with a client I know what they want and what they're looking for. I am a very good listener." In addition to these people skills, a personal shopper should be patient and capable of dealing with the long lines and customer service of department stores. You should be creative and able to come up with a variety of gift ideas. A sense of style is important, along with knowledge of the latest brands and designers. You'll need a good eye for colors and fabrics. You should also be well dressed and organized so that your client will know to trust your wardrobe suggestions.

EXPLORING

If you've spent any time at the mall, you probably already have enough shopping experience. And if you've had to buy clothes and gifts with limited funds, then you know something about budgeting. Sign up for the services of a personal shopper in a department store. In most stores the service is free, and you'll get a sense of how a shopper works. Pay close attention to the information they request from you in the beginning, then ask them later about their decision-making process. Irene Kato advises future personal shoppers to work a few years at a retail clothing store. "This way," she says, "you can observe the way people dress, what shapes and sizes we all are, how fashion trends come and go, and what stays."

EMPLOYERS

Professional men and women with high incomes and busy schedules are the primary employers of personal shoppers. Shoppers may also work with people with new jobs requiring dress clothes, but also with people who need to perk up an old wardrobe. Personal shoppers may work for executives in corporations who need to buy gifts for large staffs of employees. Some of their clients may

A personal shopper *(left)* helps a client find a shirt to complete an outfit. *(Tony Savino, The Image Works)*

be elderly or have disabilities and have problems getting out to do their shopping.

STARTING OUT

Start-up costs for personal shoppers can be very low. You may only have to invest in a computer, business cards, and a reliable form of transportation. But it could take you a very long time to develop a regular clientele. You'll want to develop the business part time while still working full time at another, more reliable job. Some of your first clients may come from your workplace. Offer free introductory services to a few people and encourage them to spread the word and hand out your business card. You'll also need to become very familiar with the local retail establishments and the discount stores with low-cost, high-quality merchandise.

"My friends and colleagues at work," Irene Kato says, "were always complimentary on what I wore and would ask where I bought my clothes, where they could find certain items, where were the best sales." Kato was taking the part-time approach to developing her personal shopping service, when downsizing at her company thrust her into the new business earlier than she'd planned. She had the opportunity to take an entrepreneurism class at a local private university, which helped her devise a business plan and taught her about the pros and cons of starting a business.

ADVANCEMENT

It takes years of dedication, quality work, and referrals to create a successful business. Personal shoppers should expect lean early years as they work to build their business and expand their clientele. After a few years of working part time and providing superior service, a personal shopper may develop his or her business into a full-time endeavor. Eventually, he or she may be able to hire an assistant to help with the administrative work, such as client billing and scheduling.

EARNINGS

Personal shoppers bill their clients in different ways. They set a regular fee for services, charge a percentage of the sale, or charge an hourly rate. They might use all these methods in their business; their billing method may depend on the client and the service. For example, when offering wardrobe consultation and shopping for clothes, a personal shopper may find it best to charge by the hour; when shopping for a small gift, it may be more reasonable to charge only a percentage. Personal shoppers charge anywhere from $25 to $125 an hour; the average hourly rate is about $75. Successful shoppers living in a large city can make between $1,500 and $3,000 a month.

Personal shoppers who work for department stores usually receive benefits such as vacation days, sick leave, health and life insurance, and a savings and pension program. Self-employed personal shoppers must provide their own benefits.

WORK ENVIRONMENT

Personal shoppers have all the advantages of owning their own business, including setting their own hours and keeping a flexible schedule. But they also have all the disadvantages, such as job insecurity and lack of benefits. "I have a bad habit of thinking about my business almost constantly," Irene Kato says. Though personal shoppers don't have to deal with the stress of a full-time office job, they will have the stress of finding new clients and keeping the business afloat entirely by themselves.

Although personal shoppers usually work from a home office, they still spend a lot of time with people, from clients to salespeople. They will obviously spend some time in department stores; if they like to shop, this can be enjoyable even when they're not buying anything for themselves. In some cases, personal shoppers visit clients' homes to advise them on their wardrobe. They do a lot of traveling, driving to a department store after a meeting with a client, then back to the client's with the goods.

OUTLOOK

Personal shopping is a new business development, so anyone embarking on the career will be taking some serious risks. There's not a lot of research available about the career, no national professional organization specifically serving personal shoppers, and no real sense of the career's future. The success of Internet commerce will probably have a big effect on the future of personal shopping. If purchasing items through the Internet becomes more commonplace, more personal shoppers will establish places for themselves on the Web. Some personal shoppers with Web sites offer consultation via email and help people purchase products online.

To attract the widest variety of clients, personal shoppers should offer as expansive a service as they can. Professional organizing is being recognized as one of the top home businesses for the future. Membership of the National Association of Professional Organizers is growing each year. *Personal assistants*, those who run errands for others, have also caught the attention of industry experts, and programs are available to assist people interested in entering this field.

FOR MORE INFORMATION

For more information on professional networking opportunities for women, contact
Executive Women International
515 South 700 East, Suite 2A
Salt Lake City, UT 84102-2855
Tel: 801-355-2800
Email: ewi@executivewomen.org
http://www.executivewomen.org

To learn about a career as a professional organizer, contact
National Association of Professional Organizers
15000 Commerce Parkway, Suite C
Mount Laurel, NJ 08054-2212
Tel: 856-380-6828
Email: napo@napo.net
http://www.napo.net

Personal Trainers

QUICK FACTS

School Subjects
Health
Physical education

Personal Skills
Communication/ideas
Helping/teaching

Work Environment
Primarily indoors
Primarily multiple locations

Minimum Education Level
Some postsecondary training

Salary Range
$15,550 to $27,680 to
$73,133+ +

Certification or Licensing
Recommended

Outlook
Much faster than the average

DOT
153

GOE
11.08.01, 14.08.01

NOC
5254

O*NET-SOC
39-9031.00

OVERVIEW

Personal trainers, often known as *fitness trainers*, assist health-conscious people with exercise, weight training, weight loss, diet and nutrition, and medical rehabilitation. During one training session, or over a period of several sessions, trainers teach their clients how to achieve their health and fitness goals. They train in the homes of their clients, their own studio spaces, or in health clubs. More than 65,000 personal trainers work in the United States, either independently or on the staff of a fitness center.

HISTORY

For much of the last half of the 20th century, "98-pound weaklings" were tempted by the Charles Atlas comic book ads to buy his workout plan and to bulk up. Atlas capitalized on a concern for good health that developed into the fitness industry after World War II. Though physical fitness has always been important to the human body, things have changed quite a bit since the days when people had to chase and hunt their own food. Before the industrial revolution, people were much more active, and the need for supplemental exercise was unnecessary. But the last century has brought easier living, laziness, and processed snack foods.

Even as early as the late 1800s, people became concerned about their health and weight and began to flock to spas and exercise camps. This proved to be a passing fad for the most part, but medical and nutritional study began to carefully explore the significance of exercise. During World War II, rehabilitation medicine proved more effective than extended rest in returning soldiers to the front line.

Even the early days of TV featured many morning segments devoted to exercise. The videotape revolution of the 1980s went hand in hand with a new fitness craze, as Jane Fonda's workout tape became a bestseller and inspired a whole industry of fitness tapes and books. Now most health clubs offer the services of personal trainers to attend to the health and fitness concerns of their members.

THE JOB

Remember the first time you ever went to the gym? The weight machines may have resembled medieval forms of torture. So, to avoid the weight training, you stuck to the treadmill. Or maybe you called upon the services of a personal trainer. Personal trainers help their clients achieve health and fitness goals. They instruct on the proper use of exercise equipment and weight machines and may suggest diet and nutrition tips.

If you've reached your own workout goals, then you may be ready to help others reach theirs. "You have to believe in working out and eating healthy," advises Emelina Edwards, a personal trainer in New Orleans. For 12 years she's been in the business of personal training, a career she chose after whipping herself into great shape at the age of 46. Now, at 58, she has a lot of first-hand experience in training, nutrition, aerobic exercise, and stress management. Edwards says, "You have to practice what you preach."

And practice Edwards does—not only does she devote time every day to her own weight training, jogging, and meditation, but she works with three to five clients in the workout facility in her home. She has a total of about 20 clients, some of whom she assists in one-on-one sessions, and others in small groups. Her clients have included men and women from the ages of 20 to 80 who are looking to improve their general physical condition or to work on specific ailments.

When meeting with a client for the first time, Edwards gets a quick history of his or her physical problems and medical conditions. "If problems are serious," Edwards says, "I check with their doctor. If mild, I explain to them what I believe will help." When she discovered that four out of five people seeking her help suffered from back problems, she did a great deal of research on back pain and how to alleviate it through exercise. "I teach people how to do for themselves," she says. "Sometimes I see a person once, or for three or four sessions, or forever."

In addition to working directly with clients, Edwards is active promoting her line of "Total Body Rejuvenation" products. These products, consisting of audiotapes and books, are based on her years of experience and the many articles she has written for fitness publications. When she's not training clients, writing articles, and selling products, she's reading fitness publications to keep up on the business, as well as speaking at public events. "When I realized I loved training," she says, "I thought of all the things I could relate to it. So along with the training, I began to write about it, and to give talks on health and fitness."

Successful personal trainers do not necessarily have to keep as busy as Edwards. They may choose to specialize in certain areas of personal training. They may work as an *athletic trainer*, helping athletes prepare for sports activities. They may specialize in helping with the rehabilitation treatment of people with injuries and other physical problems. Yoga, dance, martial arts, indoor cycling, boxing, and water fitness have all become aspects of special training programs. People call upon personal trainers to help them quit smoking, to assist with healthy pregnancies, and to maintain mental and emotional stability. Whatever the problem, whether mental or physical, people are turning to exercise and nutrition to help them deal with it.

Many personal trainers have their own studios or home gyms where they train their clients; others go into the homes of their clients. Because of the demands of the workplace, many personal trainers also work in offices and corporate fitness centers. Though most health clubs hire their own trainers to assist with club members, some hire freelance trainers as independent contractors. These independent contractors are not considered staff members and do not receive employee benefits. (IDEA Health and Fitness Association found that 30 percent of the personal trainers hired by the fitness centers surveyed were independent contractors.)

REQUIREMENTS
High School
If you are interested in health and fitness, you are probably already taking physical education classes and involved in sports activities. It is also important to take health courses and courses like home economics, which include lessons in diet and nutrition. Business courses can help you prepare for the management aspect of running your own personal training service. Science courses such as biology, chemistry, and physiology are important for your understanding of muscle groups, food and drug reactions, and other concerns of exercise science. If you are not interested in playing on sports teams, you may be able to volunteer as an assistant. These positions will allow you to learn about athletic training as well as rehabilitation treatments.

Postsecondary Training

A college education is not required to work as a personal trainer, but you can benefit from one of the many fitness-related programs offered at colleges across the country. Some relevant college programs include health education, exercise and sports science, kinesiology, fitness program management, and athletic training. These programs include courses in therapeutic exercise, nutrition, aerobics, and fitness and aging. IDEA recommends a bachelor's degree from a program that includes at least a semester each in anatomy, kinesiology, and exercise physiology. IDEA offers scholarships to students seeking careers as fitness professionals.

If you are not interested in completing a four-year program, many schools offer shorter versions of their bachelor's programs. Upon completing a shorter program, you'll receive either an associate's degree or certification from the school. Once you have established yourself in the business, continuing education courses are important for you to keep up with the advances in the industry. IDEA is one of many organizations that offer independent study courses, conferences, and seminars.

Certification or Licensing

There are so many schools and organizations that offer certification to personal trainers that it has become a concern in the industry. Without more rigid standards, the profession could suffer at the hands of less experienced, less skilled trainers. Some organizations only require membership fees and short tests for certification.

The U.S. Department of Labor reports that personal trainers must be certified in the fitness field to find employment, and health clubs look for certified trainers when hiring independent contractors. If you are seeking certification, you should choose a certifying board that offers scientifically based exams and requires continuing education credits. The American Council on Exercise, the National Federation of Professional Trainers, and American Fitness Professionals and Associates are just a few of the many groups with certification programs.

Other Requirements

Physical fitness and knowledge of health and nutrition are the most important assets of personal trainers. "The more intelligently you can speak to someone," Edwards says, "the more receptive they'll be." Your clients will also be more receptive to patience and friendliness. "I'm very enthusiastic and positive," she says regarding the way she works with her clients. You should be able to explain things clearly, recognize progress, and encourage it. You should be com-

A personal trainer teaches a client how to exercise using a Bosu ball.
(Gene Kaiser, AP Photo/South Bend Tribune)

fortable working one-on-one with people of all ages and in all physical conditions. An interest in reading fitness books and publications is important to your continuing education.

EXPLORING

Your high school may have a weight-training program, or some other extracurricular fitness program, as part of its athletic department; in addition to signing up for the program, you can assist the faculty who manage it. That way, you can learn about what goes into developing and maintaining such a program. If your school doesn't have a fitness program, seek one out at a community center, or join a health club. You should also try the services of a personal trainer. By conditioning yourself and eating a healthy diet, you'll get a good sense of the duties of a personal trainer. Any number of books and magazines address issues of health and nutrition and offer weight-training advice. The IDEA publishes several helpful health- and career-related publications including *IDEA Fitness Journal* and *IDEA Trainer Success*.

Finally, seek out part-time work at a gym or health club to meet trainers and learn about weight machines and certification programs.

EMPLOYERS

IDEA reports that there are more than 65,000 personal trainers working in the United States. Personal trainers are employed by people of all ages. Individuals hire the services of trainers, as do companies for the benefit of their employees. Though most health clubs hire personal trainers full time, some clubs hire trainers on an independent contractor basis. Sports and exercise programs at community colleges hire trainers part time to conduct classes.

Personal trainers can find clients in most major cities in all regions of the country. In addition to health clubs and corporate fitness centers, trainers find work at YMCAs, aerobics studios, and hospital fitness centers.

STARTING OUT

Most people who begin personal training do so after successful experiences with their own training. Once they've developed a good exercise regimen and healthy diet plan for themselves, they may feel ready to help others. Emelina Edwards had hit a low point in her life, and had turned to weight training to help her get through the difficult times. "I didn't have a college degree," she says, "and I needed something to do. All I had was weight training." She then called up all the women she knew, promoting her services as a personal trainer. Through the benefit of word-of-mouth, Edwards built up a clientele.

Some trainers begin by working part time or full time for health clubs and, after making connections, they go into business for themselves. As with most small businesses, personal trainers must promote themselves through classified ads, flyers posted in community centers, and other forms of advertisement. Many personal trainers have published guides on how to establish businesses.

ADVANCEMENT

After personal trainers have taken on as many individual clients as they need to maintain a business, they may choose to lead small group training sessions or conduct large aerobics classes. Some trainers join forces with other trainers to start their own fitness centers. Trainers who are employed by fitness centers may be promoted to the position of *personal training director*. These workers supervise and schedule other personal trainers and manage department budgets.

Emelina Edwards has advanced her business by venturing out into other areas of fitness instruction, such as publishing books and speaking to groups. "I want to develop more in the public speaking arena," she says. Right now, she only speaks to local groups—she'd like to go national. "I'd also like to break into the Latin market," she says. "The interest is there, and the response has been great."

EARNINGS

The IDEA reports that the average hourly rate for personal trainers is $41. Hourly fees ranged from less than $20 to $70 or more. Personal trainers who offer specialized instruction (such as in yoga, martial arts, or indoor cycling), or who work with their own clients in their own homes, can charge higher hourly rates. The U.S. Department of Labor reports that in 2007 the median annual salary for fitness trainers, which includes personal trainers, was $27,680. The lowest paid 10 percent earned $15,550 or less, and the highest paid 10 percent earned $58,990 or more. A 2008 Salary.com survey found that salaries for personal trainers ranged from less than $25,207 to $73,133 or more.

Personal trainers who work for health clubs usually receive benefits such as vacation days, sick leave, health and life insurance, and a savings and pension program. Self-employed personal trainers must provide their own benefits.

WORK ENVIRONMENT

Personal training is obviously a physically demanding job, but anybody who is in good shape and who eats a healthy diet should be able to easily handle the demands. Personal trainers who work out of their homes will enjoy familiar and comfortable surroundings. Trainers who work in a gym as independent contractors will also experience a comfortable workplace. Most good gyms maintain a cool temperature, keep the facilities clean and well-lit, and care for the weight machines. Whether in a gym or at home, personal trainers work directly with their clients, usually in one-on-one training sessions. In this teaching situation, the workplace is usually quiet and conducive to learning.

As with most self-employment, sustaining a business can be both rewarding and difficult. Many trainers appreciate being able to keep their own hours, and to work as little, or as much, as they care to. By setting their own schedules, they can arrange time for their personal workout routines. But, without an employer, there's less security, no benefits, and no steady paycheck. Personal trainers have to regularly promote their services and be ready to take on new clients.

OUTLOOK

Fitness training will continue to enjoy strong growth in the near future. The U.S. Department of Labor predicts employment opportunities for personal trainers and other fitness workers to grow much faster than the average for all occupations through 2016. As the baby boomers grow older, they will increasingly rely on the services of personal trainers. Boomers have long been interested in health and fitness, and they will carry this into their old age. A knowledge of special weight training, stretching exercises, and diets for seniors will be necessary for personal trainers in the years to come. Trainers will actively promote their services to senior centers and retirement communities.

With the number of health publications and fitness centers, people are much more knowledgeable about exercise and nutrition. This could increase business for personal trainers as people better understand the necessity of proper training and seek out professional assistance. Trainers may also be going into more of their clients homes as people set up their own workout stations complete with weights and treadmills. In the health and medical field, new developments are constantly affecting how people eat and exercise. Personal trainers must keep up with these advances, as well as any new trends in fitness and dieting.

FOR MORE INFORMATION

For information on certification, contact
American College of Sports Medicine
PO Box 1440
Indianapolis, IN 46206-1440
Tel: 317-637-9200
http://www.acsm.org

For general health and fitness topics, and to learn about certification, contact
American Council on Exercise
4851 Paramount Drive
San Diego, CA 92123-1449
Tel: 888-825-3636
Email: support@acefitness.org
http://www.acefitness.org

For information on certification, contact
American Fitness Professionals and Associates
PO Box 214
Ship Bottom, NJ 08008-0234
Tel: 800-494-7782
Email: afpa@afpafitness.com
http://www.afpafitness.com

IDEA conducts surveys, provides continuing education, and publishes books and magazines relevant to personal trainers. For information about the fitness industry in general, and personal training specifically, contact
IDEA Health and Fitness Association
10455 Pacific Center Court
San Diego, CA 92121-4339
Tel: 800-999-4332
Email: contact@ideafit.com
http://www.ideafit.com

For information on certification, contact
National Federation of Professional Trainers
PO Box 4579
Lafayette, IN 47903-4579
Tel: 800-729-6378
http://www.nfpt.com

Pet Sitters

OVERVIEW

When pet owners are on vacation or working long hours, they hire *pet sitters* to come to their homes and visit their animals. During short, daily visits, pet sitters feed the animals, play with them, clean up after them, give them medications when needed, and let them in and out of the house for exercise. *Dog walkers* may be responsible only for taking their clients' dogs out for exercise. Pet sitters may also be available for overnight stays, looking after the houses of clients as well as their pets.

HISTORY

Animals have been revered by humans for centuries, as is evidenced by early drawings on the walls of caves and tombs—cats were even considered sacred by the ancient Egyptians. Though these sacred cats may have had their own personal caretakers, it has only been within the last 10 to 15 years that pet sitting has evolved into a successful industry and a viable career option. Before groups such as the National Association of Professional Pet Sitters (NAPPS), which formed in 1989, and Pet Sitters International (PSI), which was founded in 1994, were developed, pet sitting was regarded as a way for people with spare time to make a little extra money on the side. Like babysitting, pet sitting attracted primarily teenagers and women; many children's books over the last century have depicted the trials and tribulations of young entrepreneurs in the business of pet sitting and dog walking. Patti Moran, the founder of both NAPPS and PSI, and author of *Pet Sitting for Profit*, is credited with helping pet sitters gain recognition as successful small business owners. Though many people still only pet sit occasionally for neighbors and friends, others are developing long lists of clientele and proving strong competition to kennels and boarding facilities.

THE JOB

If you live in a big city, you've seen them hit the streets with their packs of dogs. Dragged along by four or five leashes, the pet sitter walks the dogs down the busy sidewalks, allowing the animals their afternoon exercise while the pet owners are stuck in the office. You may not have realized it, but those dog walkers are probably the owners of thriving businesses. Though a hobby for some, pet sitting is for others a demanding career with many responsibilities. Michele Finley is one of these pet sitters, in the Park Slope neighborhood of Brooklyn, New York. "A lot of people seem to think pet sitting is a walk in the park (pun intended)," she says, "and go into it without realizing what it entails (again)."

For those who can't bear to leave their dogs or cats at kennels or boarders while they are away, pet sitters offer peace of mind to the owners, as well as their pets. With a pet sitter, pets can stay in familiar surroundings, as well as avoid the risks of illnesses passed on by other animals. The pets are also assured routine exercise and no disruptions in their diets. Most pet sitters prefer to work only with cats and dogs, but pet sitters are also called upon to care for birds, reptiles, gerbils, fish, and other animals.

With their own set of keys, pet sitters let themselves into the homes of their clients and care for their animals while they're away at work or on vacation. Pet sitters feed the animals, make sure they have water, and give them their medications. They clean up any messes the animals have made and clean litter boxes. They give the animals attention, playing with them, letting them outside, and taking them for walks. Usually, a pet sitter can provide pet owners with a variety of personal pet care services—they may take a pet to the vet, offer grooming, sell pet-related products, and give advice. Some pet sitters take dogs out into the country, to mountain parks, or to lakes, for exercise in wide-open spaces. "You should learn to handle each pet as an individual," Finley advises. "Just because Fluffy likes his ears scratched doesn't mean Spot does."

Pet sitters typically plan one to three visits (of 30 to 60 minutes in length) per day, or they may make arrangements to spend the night. In addition to caring for the animals, pet sitters also look after the houses of their clients. They bring in the newspapers and the mail; they water the plants; they make sure the house is securely locked. Pet sitters generally charge by the hour or per visit. They may also have special pricing for overtime, emergency situations, extra duties, and travel.

A pet sitter in Hoboken, N.J., walks her charges. *(Jeff Zelevansky, AP Photo)*

Most pet sitters work alone, without employees, no matter how demanding the work. Though this means getting to keep all the money, it also means keeping all the responsibilities. A successful pet sitting service requires a fair amount of business management. Finley works directly with the animals from 10:00 A.M. until 5:00 or 6:00 P.M., with no breaks; upon returning home, she will have five to 10 phone messages from clients. Part of her evening then consists of scheduling and rescheduling appointments, offering advice on feeding, training, and other pet care concerns, and giving referrals for boarders and vets. But despite these hours, and despite having to work holidays, as well as days when she's not feeling well, Finley appreciates many things about the job. "Being with the furries all day is the best," she says. She also likes not having to dress up for work and not having to commute to an office.

REQUIREMENTS
High School
As a pet sitter, you'll be running your own business all by yourself; therefore you should take high school courses such as accounting, marketing, and office skills. Computer science will help you learn

about the software you'll need for managing accounts and scheduling. Join a school business group that will introduce you to business practices and local entrepreneurs.

Science courses such as biology and chemistry, as well as health courses, will give you some good background for developing animal care skills. As a pet sitter, you'll be overseeing the health of the animals, their exercise, and their diets. You'll also be preparing medications and administering eye and ear drops.

As a high school student, you can easily gain hands-on experience as a pet sitter. If you know anyone in your neighborhood with pets, volunteer to care for the animals whenever the owners go on vacation. Once you've got experience and a list of references, you may even be able to start a part-time job for yourself as a pet sitter.

Postsecondary Training
Many pet sitters start their own businesses after having gained experience in other areas of animal care. Vet techs and pet shop workers may promote their animal care skills to develop a clientele for more profitable pet sitting careers. Graduates from a business college may recognize pet sitting as a great way to start a business with little overhead. But neither a vet tech qualification nor a business degree is required to become a successful pet sitter. And the only special training you need to pursue is actual experience. A local pet shop or chapter of the ASPCA may offer seminars in various aspects of animal care; the NAPPS offers a mentorship program, as well as a newsletter, while PSI sponsors correspondence programs and teleconferences.

Certification or Licensing
PSI offers the accredited pet sitter designation to applicants who pass an open book examination that covers topics in four major categories: Pet Care, Health and Nutrition, Business and Office Procedures, and Additional Services. Accreditation must be renewed every three years. The National Association of Professional Pet Sitters offers the certified pet sitter designation to applicants who complete a home-study course and pass an examination. Certification tells prospective clients that you have met industry standards, and may increase your chances of being hired.

Michele Finley has a different view on certification. "I really don't think such things are necessary," she says. "All you need to know can be learned by working for a good sitter and reading pet health and behavioral newsletters."

Though there is no particular pet-sitting license required of pet sitters, insurance protection is important. Liability insurance protects the pet sitter from lawsuits; both the NAPPS and PSI offer group liability packages to its members. Pet sitters must also be bonded. Bonding assures the pet owners that if anything is missing from their homes after a pet sitting appointment, they can receive compensation immediately.

Other Requirements

You must love animals and animals must love you. But this love for animals can't be your only motivation—keep in mind that, as a pet sitter, you'll be in business for yourself. You won't have a boss to give you assignments, and you won't have a secretary or bookkeeper to do the paperwork. You also won't have employees to take over on weekends, holidays, and days when you're not feeling well. Though some pet sitters are successful enough to afford assistance, most must handle all the aspects of their businesses by themselves. So, you should be self-motivated, and as dedicated to the management of your business as you are to the animals.

Pet owners entrust you with the care of their pets and their homes, so you must be trustworthy and reliable. You should also be organized and prepared for emergency situations. And not only must you be patient with the pets and their owners, but also with the development of your business: It will take a few years to build up a good list of clients.

As a pet sitter, you must also be ready for the dirty work—you'll be cleaning litter boxes and animal messes within the house. On dog walks, you'll be picking up after them on the street. You may be giving animals medications. You'll also be cleaning aquariums and bird cages.

"Work for an established pet sitter to see how you like it," Finley advises. "It's a very physically demanding job and not many can stand it for long on a full-time basis." Pet sitting isn't for those who just want a nine-to-five desk job. Your day will be spent moving from house to house, taking animals into backyards, and walking dogs around the neighborhoods. Though you may be able to develop a set schedule for yourself, you really will have to arrange your work hours around the hours of your clients. Some pet sitters start in the early morning hours, while others only work afternoons or evenings. To stay in business, a pet sitter must be prepared to work weekends, holidays, and long hours in the summertime.

EXPLORING

There are many books, newsletters, and magazines devoted to pet care. *Pet Sitting for Profit* (Howell Book House, 2006), by Patti Moran,

The Most Popular Pets in the U.S.

Freshwater Fish:	142.0 million
Cats:	88.3 million
Dogs:	74.8 million
Small Animals (hamsters, gerbils, ferrets, etc.):	24.3 million
Birds:	16.0 million
Horses:	13.8 million
Reptiles:	13.4 million
Saltwater Fish:	9.6 million

Source: 2007–2008 *National Pet Owners Survey*, by total number owned

is just one of many books that can offer insight into pet sitting as a career. Magazines such as *The WORLD of Professional Pet Sitting* (http://www.petsit.com/media/publication_professional.php) can also teach you about the requirements of professional animal care. And many books discuss the ins and outs of small business ownership.

Try pet sitting for a neighbor or family member to get a sense of the responsibilities of the job. Some pet sitters hire assistants on an independent contractor basis; contact an area pet sitter listed in the phone book or with one of the professional organizations, and see if you can "hire on" for a day or two. Not only will you learn firsthand the duties of a pet sitter, but you'll also see how the business is run.

EMPLOYERS

Nearly all pet sitters are self-employed, although a few may work for other successful pet sitters who have built up a large enough clientele to require help. It takes most pet sitters an appreciable period of time to establish a business substantial enough to make a living without other means of income. However, the outlook for this field is excellent, and start-up costs are minimal, making it a good choice for animal lovers who want to work for themselves. For those who have good business sense and a great deal of ambition, the potential for success is good.

STARTING OUT

You're not likely to find job listings under "pet sitter" in the newspaper. Most pet sitters schedule all their work themselves. However, you may find ads in the classifieds or in weekly community papers from pet owners looking to hire pet sitters. Some people who become pet sitters have backgrounds in animal care—they may have worked for vets, breeders, or pet shops. These people enter the business with a client list already in hand, having made contacts with many pet owners. But, if you're just starting out in animal care, you need to develop a list of references. This may mean volunteering your time to friends and neighbors, or working very cheaply. If you're willing to actually stay in the house while the pet owners are on vacation, you should be able to find plenty of pet sitting opportunities in the summertime. Post your name, phone number, and availability on the bulletin boards of grocery stores, colleges, and coffee shops around town. Once you've developed a list of references, and have made connections with pet owners, you can start expanding, and increasing your profits.

Susan Clark runs a professional dog-walking business in Brooklyn, New York. She suggests another way of breaking into the business. "I started my business," she says, "by visiting pet stores and asking if they would supply me with their mailing lists. In return, when I went door to door with my own postcards, I would include their business cards. Many pet store owners were kind enough to agree to this arrangement. I have to say though, the majority of my business came from two other sources: word-of-mouth and referrals from other dog walkers in the neighborhood. I knew a great deal of dog owners in the area because I would go to the dog runs with my own two dogs. The minute I mentioned I was thinking about opening up a dog-walking service, I was in business. My dog walker and boarder were incredibly supportive and also sent business my way. I was very fortunate, and have never forgotten their generosity so I do the same for other new dog walkers in the neighborhood."

ADVANCEMENT

Your advancement will be a result of your own hard work. The more time you dedicate to your business, the bigger the business will become. The success of any small business can be very unpredictable. For some, a business can build very quickly, for others it may take years. Some pet sitters start out part time, perhaps even volunteering, then may find themselves with enough business to quit their full-time jobs and devote themselves entirely to pet sitting. Once your business takes off, you may be able to afford an assistant, or an entire staff. Some pet sitters even have franchises across the country. You may even choose to develop your business into a much larger operation, such as a dog day care facility.

EARNINGS

Pet sitters set their own prices, charging by the visit, the hour, or the week. They may also charge consultation fees, and additional fees on holidays. They may have special pricing plans in place, such as for emergency situations or for administering medications. Depending on the kinds of animals (sometimes pet sitters charge less to care for cats than dogs), pet sitters generally charge between $8 and $15 for a 30-minute visit. The average per-visit rate is $13.20, according to Pet Sitters International. PSI conducted a survey of annual salaries and discovered that the range was too great to determine a median. Some very successful pet sitters have annual salaries of more than $100,000, while others only make $5,000 a year. Though a pet sitter can make a good profit in any area of the country, a bigger city will offer more clients. Pet sitters in their first five years of business are unlikely to make more than $10,000 a year; pet sitters who have had businesses for eight years or more may make more than $40,000 a year.

Pet sitters who work for a company usually receive benefits such as health and life insurance, sick leave, vacation days, and a savings and pension plan. Self-employed pet sitters must provide their own benefits.

WORK ENVIRONMENT

Some pet sitters prefer to work close to their homes; Michele Finley only walks dogs in her Brooklyn neighborhood. In a smaller town, however, pet sitters have to do a fair amount of driving from place to place. Depending on the needs of the animals, the pet sitter will let the pets outside for play and exercise. Although filling food and water bowls and performing other chores within the house is generally peaceful work, walking dogs on busy city sidewalks can be stressful. And in the wintertime, you'll spend a fair amount of time out in the inclement weather. "Icy streets are murder," Finley says. "And I don't like dealing with people who hate dogs and are always yelling to get the dog away from them."

Though you'll have some initial interaction with pet owners when getting house keys, taking down phone numbers, and meeting the pets and learning about their needs, most of your work will be alone with the animals. But you won't be totally isolated. If dog walking in the city, you'll meet other dog owners and other people in the neighborhood.

OUTLOOK

Pet sitting as a small business is expected to skyrocket in the coming years. Most pet sitters charge fees comparable to kennels and boarders, but some charge less. And many pet owners prefer to leave their pets in the house, rather than take the pets to unfamiliar locations. This has made pet sitting a desirable and cost-effective alternative to other pet care situations. Pet sitters have been successful in cities both large and small. In the last few years, pet sitting has been featured in the *Wall Street Journal* and other national publications. *Woman's Day* magazine listed pet sitting as one of the top-grossing businesses for women.

Because a pet sitting business requires little money to start up, many more people may enter the business hoping to make a tidy profit. This could lead to heavier competition; it could also hurt the reputation of pet sitting if too many irresponsible and unprepared people run bad businesses. But if pet owners remain cautious when hiring pet sitters, the unreliable workers will have trouble maintaining clients.

FOR MORE INFORMATION

For information about pet care, contact
American Society for the Prevention of Cruelty to Animals
424 East 92nd Street
New York, NY 10128-6804
Tel: 212-876-7700
http://www.aspca.org

For information on pet setting and certification, contact
National Association of Professional Pet Sitters
15000 Commerce Parkway, Suite C
Mt. Laurel, NJ 08054-2212
Tel: 856-439-0324
Email: napps@ahint.com
http://www.petsitters.org

For certification, careers, and small business information, as well as general information about pet sitting, contact
Pet Sitters International
201 East King Street
King, NC 27021-9161
Tel: 336-983-9222
Email: info@petsit.com
http://www.petsit.com

━━━━━━━━━━━━━━━━━━━ **INTERVIEW** ━━━━━━━━━━━━━━━━━━

Darlene Ehlers is the owner of Pampered Pets Home Care in Blue Jay, Ohio. She discussed her career with the editors of Careers in Focus: Entrepreneurs.

Q. Tell us about your work as a pet sitter.

A. I started my business in July 1997 after reading an article about pet sitting. I purchased the reference book *Pet Sitting for Profit,* by Patti Moran of Pet Sitters International. At the time I was working full time and thought this might be a fun way to earn some additional income. Never did I believe (but hoped) that someday it would turn into a full-time job at which I could support myself. I started slowly and followed the guidelines in Patti's book. I also met with other pet sitters and the local small business administration office for some pointers.

I work out of my home and have a room set up as an office. As a pet sitter I usually try to stay within a 10-mile radius from my home. I live in the suburban community of Blue Jay, Ohio, outside of Cincinnati. This is a pretty rural community with mostly single-family homes.

I advertise in local newspapers and on bulletin boards in local pet shops, grocery stores, etc. In the beginning most of my business was obtained by advertising in a small free bulletin that was available to the public. After awhile my business was based on referrals from veterinarians, customers, other pet sitters, and friends.

After an initial contact from a perspective customer, I send them an informational brochure about my company. If they are still interested in using a pet sitter, I make arrangements to meet with them and their pets for a contract visit. This is a complimentary visit at which time I provide them with a folder including the contract as well as other forms and paperwork that I have developed.

After getting all of the pertinent information regarding their pet(s), I obtain a key and finalize the dates with the customer. A few days prior to my starting my visits, I send the customer an assignment confirmation form with all the information about when to start and end my visits.

I take care of a variety of animals and perform a variety of tasks, including:

• Dogs: Visits with dogs normally consists of three or four visits per day. During the A.M./P.M. visits I wash their bowls, give them fresh food and water, take them for a walk or let them out in the yard to go potty and play. I also take in the mail and take the trash out to the curb on collection day. I water any inside plants; adjust blinds and lights to give the house that lived in appearance. I have some jobs that if my schedule is not too busy I will sit with the dog and watch TV. I actually had one customer who would call me up and ask me to go over and give the dogs their nightly ice cream at 8:00 P.M. because they wouldn't be home in time.

- Cats: Clean litter boxes, wash food/water bowls, give fresh water and food. Play, pet, and cuddle.
- Horses: Clean stalls, turn horses out into pasture, wash out buckets, and give fresh water. Feed grain and hay. Put horses back in barn overnight. Grooming is optional and an additional charge is incurred.
- Birds: Clean cages, wash out food/water dishes, and give fresh water/food.

As with any pet, they sometimes have accidents or get sick. If this happens I clean up the messes and can administer any medication as long as I check with the veterinarian first to get his or her approval.

Q. What are some of the most interesting things that have happened to you as a pet sitter?

A. I've been pretty lucky and haven't had any pet emergencies. I did lock myself in the garage one day with three dogs. My keys were in the house. I finally decided to put all three dogs in the car that was in the garage so that I could open the garage door. (I remembered that I just finished letting the dogs out in the backyard and the back door was still unlocked.) When I got the third dog in the car the garage door started to open without me pushing any buttons! I looked outside to see if the customer had come home early, but there was nobody there. I went around and let myself back in the house and then let the dogs out of the car. I noticed that the garage door opener was on the seat. One of the dogs must have opened the garage door for me!

I had a customer who had two wonderful labs. The customer would call me and ask me to stop by and give the dogs their 8:00 ice cream treat, which they got every night. They would each get a little cup of vanilla ice cream and would sit there very quietly slurping it out of the container.

I took care of a cat that had a feeding tube inserted into his stomach. He was a very sweet cat and very patient. He required medicine first to make sure he didn't get an upset stomach. He seemed to know when I was there to take care of him. He'd follow me around while I got everything ready and then sit on my lap patiently while I gave him his medicine. Then he would jump down somehow knowing that he needed to wait 30 minutes before his feeding would begin. He would show up just about that time and again sit on my lap patiently for an hour while his food and other meds were administered. Most of the time he would fall fast asleep on my lap. When it was all over, he had the look on his face of a very content and happy kitty.

Probably the most interesting thing that ever happened was when I got word from Pet Sitters International that I had won Pet Sitter of the Year! It had been a dream of mine for some nine years.

Q. What are some of the pros and cons of your job?

A. Pros: Being your own boss, wet noses and sloppy kisses, walking dogs in the fresh air and sunshine. Appreciating all the seasons, even the snow in the wintertime. Meeting a new breed of dog or cat that you hadn't sat for previously. You are able to cuddle with so many wonderful animals. Having customers and their pets like and appreciate you. Setting up your own office and relaxing while you are doing paperwork. Being able to make your own schedule. Not having to sit in a cubicle all day. Being part of Pet Sitters International and meeting so many other wonderful pet sitters who have become friends. Being able to take care of a sick animal. Keeping in shape due to walking dogs. Being able to dress in jeans, shorts, and other comfortable attire. Realizing that you get back what you put into your business and really loving what you do. Even after returning from a vacation when your spouse tells you he hates going back to work, you stop and think, hey I can't wait to get back to the animals. Everyday is like a vacation. Being able to support yourself while pet sitting.

Cons: Having to be out in all kinds of weather; driving sometimes 100+ miles a day; working weekends, nights, and holidays; meeting a new customer and hoping that they like you; and trying to find time to juggle sitting, paperwork, personal life, and checking the schedule over and over to make sure you didn't miss anything.

Q. What are the most important personal and professional qualities for pet sitters?

A. You need to present yourself both personally and on the job as a professional. This means that you dress in a professional manner and have a neat appearance. I've had customers ask me if I was part of a franchise since my presentation is so professional. You need to be able to carry on a conversation with a potential customer and be honest if you don't know how to answer a question. If you have advertising on your car, then your car should always be clean (or as often as possible). You need to be courteous to people and let them tell you how they want you to care for their pets. You need to be dedicated, honest, loyal, detail oriented, and have a true love of animals. You need to keep all appointments timely and return calls promptly. A good judge of character is also a good thing as well as knowing your breeds and their temperaments.

Swimming Pool Servicers

QUICK FACTS

School Subjects
Chemistry
Technical/shop

Personal Skills
Following instructions
Technical/scientific

Work Environment
Indoors and outdoors
Primarily multiple locations

Minimum Education Level
High school diploma

Salary Range
$20,000 to $40,000 to
$50,000+

Certification or Licensing
Voluntary

Outlook
About as fast as the average

DOT
891

GOE
11.07.01

NOC
7441

O*NET-SOC
N/A

OVERVIEW

Swimming pool servicers clean, adjust, and perform minor repairs on swimming pools, hot tubs, and auxiliary equipment. There are millions of pools across the country in hotels, parks, apartment complexes, health clubs, and other public areas. These public pools are required by law to be regularly serviced by trained technicians. In addition, the number of homeowners with personal pools is increasing, and these private pools also need professional servicing.

HISTORY

Swimming for enjoyment and physical activity is as old as walking and running. Swimming pools date back to the bathhouses in the palaces of ancient Greece. These bathhouses were elaborate spas, complete with steam rooms, saunas, and large pools. But swimming was a popular pastime even among those who didn't have access to bathhouses; many swam in the rivers, oceans, and the lakes of the world. The plagues of medieval Europe made people cautious about swimming in unclean waters, but soon swimming regained popularity. Swimmers swam with their heads above water in a style developed when people were still afraid of water contamination. This swimming style changed in the mid-1800s when American Indians introduced an early version of the modern "crawl." Swimming in natural spring waters was even recommended as a health benefit, inspiring hospitals and spas to develop around hot springs.

The first modern Olympics held in Athens featured swimming as one of the nine competitions. Swimming as both a sport and a pastime has continued to develop along with the technology of pool maintenance. By the 1960s, the National Swimming Pool Foundation had evolved to support research in pool safety and the education of pool operators.

THE JOB

Swimming pool servicers travel a regularly scheduled route, visiting several pools a day. They keep pools clean and equipment operating properly. In general, a pool that receives routine maintenance develops fewer problems.

Mark Randall owns a pool service business in Malibu, California. "My tools range from a tile brush to a state-of-the-art computer and printer," he says. Randall has two employees, so his day usually starts with phone calls to his crew and customers. "Then I go out and clean a few of the more difficult accounts," he says.

Cleaning is one of the regular duties of pool servicers. Leaves and other debris need to be scooped off the surface of the water with a net on a long pole. To clean beneath the surface, servicers use a special vacuum cleaner on the pool floor and walls. They scrub pool walls, tiles, and gutters around the pool's edge with stainless steel or nylon brushes to remove layers of grit and scum that collect at the water line. They also hose down the pool deck and unclog the strainers that cover the drains.

After cleaning the pool and its surroundings, servicers test the bacterial content and pH balance (a measure of acidity and alkalinity) of the water. While the tests are simple and take only a few minutes, they are very important. A sample of the pool water is collected in a jar and a few drops of a testing chemical are added to the water. This chemical causes the water to change colors, indicating the water's chemical balance. Swimming pool servicers use these results to determine the amount of chlorine and other chemicals that should be added to make the water safe. The chemicals often used, which include potassium iodide, hydrochloric acid, sodium carbonate, chlorine, and others, are poured directly into the pool or added through a feeder device in the circulation system. These chemicals, when properly regulated, kill bacteria and algae that grow in water. However, high levels of chemicals can cause eye or skin irritation. As a result, pool servicers must wear gloves and use caution when working. Because the chemical makeup of every pool is different and can change daily or even hourly, servicers keep accurate records of the levels of chemicals added to the pool during their visit. Pool owners or managers take up the responsibility of testing the water between visits from the servicer. Home pools usually have their water tested a few times a week, but large public pools are tested hourly.

Swimming pool servicers also inspect and perform routine maintenance on pool equipment, such as circulation pumps, filters, and heaters. To clean a filter, servicers force water backwards through it to dislodge any debris that has accumulated. They make sure there are no leaks in pipes, gaskets, connections, or other parts. If a drain or pipe is clogged, servicers use a steel snake, plunger, or other plumbing tool to clear it. They also adjust thermostats, pressure gauges, and other controls to make the pool water comfortable. Minor repairs to machinery, such as fixing or replacing small components, may be necessary. When major repairs are needed, servicers first inform the pool owner before making any repairs.

"An accomplished pool tech," Randall says, "can do a pool in about 20 minutes. Most pool techs would do this 10 to 20 times a day."

Another major task for swimming pool servicers in most regions of the country is closing outdoor pools for the winter. In the fall, servicers drain the water out of the pool and its auxiliary equipment. Openings into the pool are plugged, and all pool gear, such as diving boards, ladders, and pumps, is removed, inspected, and stored. The pool is covered with a tarpaulin and tied or weighted in place. In warmer climates where water does not freeze, pools are usually kept full and treated with special chemicals through the winter.

Extra work is also required when a pool is reopened in the spring. After the pool is uncovered and the tank and pool deck are swept clean, swimming pool servicers inspect for cracks, leaks, loose tiles, and broken lamps. They repair all minor problems and make recommendations to the owner about any major work they feel is necessary, such as painting the interior of the pool. Equipment removed in the fall, such as ladders and diving boards, is cleaned and installed. Servicers test water circulation and heating systems to make sure they are operating properly, and then fill the pool with water. Once filled, the pool water is tested and the appropriate chemicals are added to make it safe for swimming.

For every job, servicers keep careful records of the maintenance work they have done so they can inform the company and the customer.

REQUIREMENTS

High School

Take science courses such as chemistry and biology to gain understanding of the chemicals used in testing pool water. Shop courses with lessons in electrical wiring and motors will help you develop skills for repairing and servicing machines and equipment. Bookkeeping and accounting courses are also helpful to learn how to keep financial and tax records. You should also learn about spreadsheet and database software programs because you will probably use computers to maintain files on profits and expenses, customers, equipment, and employees. Finally, serving as an assistant on a swim team can teach you firsthand about the requirements of maintaining a regulation pool.

Postsecondary Training

You can gain most of the technical training that you will need for this career on the job. By working with another trained professional, you'll learn the basics of pool maintenance within a few months. However, if you are considering running your own business, prepare yourself further by enrolling in college courses in sales, math, accounting, and small business management.

Mark Randall has had college and technical training in various fields and has worked as a mechanic, data analyst, and prop builder for a movie studio. "I had no idea I would end up in the pool business," he says. "Luckily, my background was actually very good training for my current business." He recommends that people interested in pool maintenance take advanced courses in electrical applications, electronics, plumbing, and hydraulics.

Certification and Licensing

Randall believes that certification and licensing are very important to running a professional outfit. He is certified by the health department, has a business license, and belongs to the Independent Pool and Spa Service Organization. Certification is available from the National Swimming Pool Foundation, the Association of Pool & Spa Professionals, and by service franchisers. Certification programs consist of a set number of classroom hours and a written exam. While not a requirement, certification does indicate that you've reached a certain level of expertise and skill and can help you promote your business.

Other Requirements

Because servicers often work alone with minimum supervision, it is important that you have self-discipline and a responsible attitude.

Swimming Pool Stats, 2006

In-Ground Pools

Number Installed:	.8 million
Most Popular States:	California, Florida, Texas, Arizona, and New York
Average Age of Owner:	45+
Average Income of Owner:	$50,000+

Above-Ground Pools

Number Installed:	3.7 million
Most Popular States:	New York, California, New Jersey, Pennsylvania, and Illinois
Average Age of Owner:	35 to 54
Average Income of Owner:	$25,000–$100,000

Hot Tubs

Number Installed:	5.6 million
Most Popular States:	California, Florida, Texas, Washington, and Arizona
Average Age of Owner:	35 to 54
Average Income of Owner:	$75,000+

Source: Association of Pool & Spa Professionals

Inner drive and ambition will determine the success of your business as you work to attract new clients.

"Persistence is probably the most important quality," Randall says. He also emphasizes a strong work ethic and good communication skills. You'll also need to keep up with the technology of swimming pool maintenance to stay knowledgeable about new equipment and services available to your clients.

EXPLORING

A summer or part-time job with a school, park district, community center, or local health club can provide you with opportunities to learn more about servicing swimming pools. Hotels, motels, apartment buildings, and condominium complexes also frequently have pools and may hire summer or part-time workers to service them. Such a job could offer firsthand insight into the duties of swimming pool servicers, as well as help in obtaining full-time employment with a pool maintenance company later.

EMPLOYERS

A majority of swimming pool servicers are self-employed. With nearly 8.6 million residential swimming pools in the country, pool service owners can find clients in practically every neighborhood. In addition to servicing residential pools, workers service the pools of motels, apartment complexes, and public parks.

Some servicers choose to work with a franchise service company. These franchisers often offer training and usually provide an established client base.

STARTING OUT

Once servicers have the training and the money to invest in equipment, they work on pursuing clients. This may involve promoting their business through advertising, flyers, and word-of-mouth. They may be able to get referrals from local pool and spa construction companies.

"I started out riding with a friend who worked for a large pool service company," Mark Randall says, "and I learned as much as I could. After that, I found a small route for sale." Randall borrowed money from the bank to buy the established route of customers, then used his training to start servicing pools. "It was sink or swim, pardon the pun," he says. "But I worked very hard the first couple of years and have been fairly successful."

ADVANCEMENT

Advancement is usually shown through a growth in business. More area pool construction, positive feedback from customers, and some years in the business will attract more clients and more routes to service. If a business does really well, swimming pool servicers may choose to hire additional employees to do most of the service work, allowing more time to focus on office work and administrative details. Servicers may also expand their business to include the sale of pools, spas, and maintenance equipment.

After many years in the business, Randall is debating his next career move. "I'm toying with the idea of getting a contractor's license," he says, "and building pools."

EARNINGS

The amount of money swimming pool servicers make depends upon the region of the country in which they work (which determines the length of the swimming season), services provided by the business, and levels of experience. Experts in the business estimate that an experienced pool service owner can average $40,000 to $50,000 a year. Beginning servicers just starting to build a clientele or those that work in an area of the country that allows for only a few months of swimming may earn less than $20,000 a year.

Since swimming pool servicers operate their own businesses, they are typically responsible for providing their own insurance and retirement plans.

WORK ENVIRONMENT

Swimming pool servicers generally work alone and sometimes have little client contact. Most of the work is not particularly strenuous, though kneeling, bending, and carrying equipment from a van to the pool is necessary. Servicers work both indoors and outdoors and usually work in pleasant weather. They must handle chemicals, requiring the use of protective gloves and possibly a breathing mask to guard against fumes.

Pool servicing can be an excellent job for those who enjoy spending time outside. "I find cleaning pools to be kind of relaxing," Mark Randall says, "and a good time to enjoy my surroundings. Some people find it boring and monotonous. I guess you just need a good perspective."

OUTLOOK

According to the Association of Pool & Spa Professionals, pool sales are increasing nationwide. In 1993, there were 2.9 million in-ground pools and 2.1 million above-ground pools. By 2006, those numbers rose to 4.8 million and 3.7 million, respectively. Industry experts attribute this growth to increasing wealth among homeowners, a growing desire to enhance and alter existing homes, and a general rise in the standard of living.

With the growing number of pools, the demand for professionals trained to maintain and repair them will be strong. In addition, with more homeowners installing personal pools, there is growing concern for pool safety. The establishment of pool laws benefits servicers because they are often hired to help owners meet and keep up with safety regulations. An increased awareness among pool owners about the need to keep pools and hot tubs clean to prevent infection will continue to keep servicers in business.

Technological developments will also create more work for servicers. The need to maintain and repair new equipment, such as solar heaters, automatic timers, pool covers, and chemical dispensers, will keep pool services in demand.

FOR MORE INFORMATION

For information on education and certification programs, contact the following organizations:

Association of Pool & Spa Professionals
2111 Eisenhower Avenue
Alexandria, VA 22314-4695
Tel: 703-838-0083
http://apsp.org

National Swimming Pool Foundation
4775 Granby Circle
Colorado Springs, CO 80919-3131
Tel: 719-540-9119
http://www.nspf.com

To learn about scholarship opportunities, contact
Independent Pool and Spa Service Association
PO Box 15828
Long Beach, CA 90815-0828
Tel: 888-360-9505
Email: ipssamail@aol.com
http://www.ipssa.com

To read about issues affecting the swimming pool industry, visit the AQUA Magazine *Web page, or contact it for subscription information.*
AQUA Magazine
Email: circ@aquamagazine.com
http://www.aquamagazine.com

Wedding and Party Consultants

QUICK FACTS

School Subjects
Family and consumer science
Music
Theater/dance

Personal Skills
Communication/ideas
Leadership/management

Work Environment
Indoors and outdoors
Primarily multiple locations

Minimum Education Level
High school diploma

Salary Range
$25,000 to $60,000 to
$100,000+

Certification or Licensing
Recommended

Outlook
Faster than the average

DOT
299

GOE
11.01.01

NOC
6481

O*NET-SOC
N/A

OVERVIEW

From directing the bride to the best dress shops and cake decorators to pinning on the corsages the day of the wedding, *wedding and party consultants,* sometimes called *event professionals,* assist in the planning of weddings, receptions, and other large celebrations and events. These consultants generally have home-based businesses, but they spend a great deal of time visiting vendors and reception and wedding sites.

HISTORY

Weddings have long provided good careers for musicians, photographers, florists, printers, caterers, and others. Even marriage "brokers"—men and women who made their livings pairing up brides with grooms for nicely "arranged" marriages—were once considered prominent members of some cultures. Wedding consulting, however, has only emerged in recent years. In the years before wedding consultants, brides divided up responsibilities among cousins and aunts—a family got together to lick invitation envelopes factory-line style, a favorite aunt mixed batches of butter mints, a married sister with some recent wedding experience helped the bride pick a dress and china pattern. But usually it wasn't until after the event that the bride really had a sense of how to plan a wedding. Enter the first serious wedding consultants in the early 1980s. Recognizing how a bride can benefit a great deal from a knowledgeable guide, men and women hired themselves out as wedding and party experts. But it's only been in the last few years that the major wedding magazines and publications have given serious consideration to wedding consultants. Now most wedding experts consider a consultant a necessity in planning a perfect and cost-efficient wedding.

THE JOB

Can't decide whether to have butterflies or doves released at your wedding? Want to get married on a boat, but don't know how to arrange it? Want a chef who will prepare your reception dinner tableside? Even if your requests are a little more mainstream than these, it can be difficult choosing reliable florists and other vendors and staying within a budget. The average wedding costs close to $30,000 (including the dress), but many brides end up frustrated and disappointed with their ceremonies. Wedding consultants help brides save money and avoid stress by offering their services at the earliest stages of planning. They provide the bride with cost estimates, arrange for ceremony and reception sites, order invitations, and help select music. They also offer advice on wedding etiquette and tradition. Consultants then stay on call for their brides right through the ceremonies and receptions, pinning on flowers, instructing ushers and other members of the wedding parties, taking gifts from guests, and organizing the cake-cutting and bouquet toss.

When brides and their families seek out the services of Packy Boukis, owner of Only You Wedding and Event Consulting, she offers them "The Love Story," a full-service package of planning and organization. "I create a binder for the bride," Boukis explains. "It includes a wedding schedule, the wedding party, a section for each vendor, a budget. Everything she'll need is in that book, and it's updated every four to six weeks." In these cases, Boukis helps the bride with every step of the planning. She goes with the bride to visit each vendor, such as florists and photographers, to offer her advice and negotiate prices. Boukis is also present at the rehearsal and the wedding to organize and see to the last-minute details, assisting in everything from floral arrangement to sewing on popped buttons. Boukis has a full office in her home and works alone, with the exception of the wedding day when she has the assistance of a small staff and her husband. "My husband meets with the groomsmen," Boukis says, "and makes sure the tuxes are okay."

Despite her involvement in the many different stages of a wedding's plan, Boukis is quick to point out that each wedding is still very much the bride's own. "I show her three different vendors for each category," she says. "I don't dictate; it's her choice." It is Boukis's responsibility as consultant to make sure that the bride has a stress-free event, and to help the bride save money. Boukis benefits from discounts on services and accepts no commissions or rebates, therefore passing savings on to the brides.

In addition to full-service consulting, Boukis offers smaller, less-expensive packages. The "First Date" package is simply a single consultation, while the "I Do, I Do" package includes only wedding day assistance with the plans the bride has already made herself.

Though Boukis will sell invitations from time to time, she doesn't market products. Some consultants, however, sell a variety of things from candles and linens to calligraphic invitations to party favors. A consultant may even own a complete bridal boutique. Some consultants specialize in only "destination" weddings. They set up services in exotic locales, like Hawaii, and handle all the details for an out-of-town bride who will only be arriving the week of the wedding. Consultants also arrange for special wedding sites like historic homes, public gardens, and resorts.

A consultant can also introduce a bride to a number of "extras" that she may not have been aware of before. In addition to arranging for the flowers, candles, and cakes, a consultant may arrange for horse-and-carriage rides, doves to be released after the ceremony, wine bars for the reception, goldfish in bowls at the tables, and other frills. Some brides rely on consultants to meet difficult requests, such as booking special kinds of musicians, or finding alternatives to flowers. Weddings on TV and in the movies often inspire brides; a candlelit wedding on the TV show *Friends* in a condemned, half-demolished church sent wedding consultants scurrying to recreate the site in their own cities.

REQUIREMENTS
High School
To be a wedding consultant, you have to know about more than wedding traditions and etiquette. Above all, wedding consulting is a business, so take courses in accounting and business management. A bride will be relying on you to stay well within her budget, so you'll need to be able to balance a checkbook and work with figures. A sense of style is also very important in advising a bride on colors, flowers, and decorations—take art courses and courses in design. A home economics course may offer lessons in floral arrangement, menu planning, fashion, tailoring, and other subjects of use to a wedding planner.

Practically any school organization will offer you a lot of experience in leadership and planning. Also, join your prom and homecoming committees, and various school fundraising events. You'll develop budgeting skills, while also learning about booking bands, photographers, and other vendors.

Postsecondary Training

A good liberal arts education can be valuable to a wedding consultant, but isn't necessary. Community college courses in small business operation can help you learn about marketing and bookkeeping. Some colleges offer courses in event planning. Courses in art and floral design are valuable, and you should take computer courses to learn how to use databases and graphics programs. Your best experience is going to be gained by actually planning weddings, which may not happen until after you've received some referrals from a professional organization. Various professional organizations offer home study programs, conferences, and seminars for wedding consultants. You should speak to representatives of the organizations to learn more about their programs, and to determine which one would be best for you. The Association of Bridal Consultants (ABC) has an informal apprenticeship program that links new members with established consultants. The Association of Certified Professional Wedding Consultants also offers a training program, which addresses such topics as starting a business and dealing with contracts and fees.

Certification or Licensing

Certification isn't required to work as a consultant, but it can help you build your business quickly. ABC offers certification via its Professional Development Program, a home-study program that includes courses in etiquette, marketing, and planning. The Association of Certified Professional Wedding Consultants, Weddings Beautiful Worldwide (a subsidiary of the National Bridal Service), and June Wedding Inc. also offer certification. Packy Boukis received certification from June Wedding Inc., an organization from which she also received her first clients. Brides often contact professional associations directly, and the associations refer the brides to certified consultants in their area. Upon completing any of the training programs mentioned above, you'll receive some form of certification. Higher levels of certification exist for those who have been certified longer.

Other Requirements

From parties to vacations, Boukis loves to organize things. "You should be creative," she advises, "and like to help people." Good people skills are very important—much of your success will rely on your relationships with vendors, musicians, and all the others you'll

A wedding planner *(left)* discusses arrangements with a future bride *(center)* and her mother. *(Stanley Walker, The Image Works/Syracuse Newspapers)*

be hiring for weddings, as well as good word-of-mouth from previous clients. You should be good at helping people make decisions; moving clients in the right direction will be a very important part of your job. Patience is necessary, as you'll need to create a stress-free environment for the bride.

EXPLORING

Modern Bride, and other bridal magazines, publish many articles on wedding planning, traditions, and trends. Subscribe to a bridal magazine to get a sense of all the ins and outs of wedding consulting. Visit the Web sites of professional associations, as well as posting sites like Boukis's at "Cleveland Live." Sites featuring questions and answers from professionals can give you a lot of insight into the business. A few cable networks feature series on weddings; for example, *Whose Wedding Is It Anyway?* on the Style channel depicts wedding planning documentary style.

For more hands-on experience, contact the professional organizations for the names of consultants in your area and pay them a visit. Some consultants hire assistants occasionally to help with large weddings. A part-time job with a florist, caterer, or photographer can also give you a lot of experience in wedding planning.

EMPLOYERS

Most consultants are self-employed. In addition to working for brides and other individuals planning large celebrations, consultants hire on with museums and other nonprofit organizations to plan fundraising events. They also work for retail stores to plan sales events and organize grand-opening events for new businesses. Hotels, resorts, and restaurants that host a number of weddings sometimes hire consultants in full-time staff positions. Large retail stores also hire their own full-time events coordinators.

Consultants work all across the country, but are most successful in large cities. In an urban area, a consultant may be able to fill every weekend with at least one wedding. Consultants for "destination" weddings settle in popular vacation and wedding spots such as Hawaii, the Bahamas, and Las Vegas.

STARTING OUT

Packy Boukis worked for several years in other businesses before finding her way to self-employment. "But all my jobs," she says, "led naturally to consulting." Early on, she worked in her family's chocolate company, Mageros Candies, which gave her a strong entrepreneurial background. She holds an associate degree in business administration, and has worked as an executive secretary and as a teacher. It was demonstrating magnetic windows for Sears that helped her develop valuable sales, presentation, and people skills. She has also worked for a bridal registry in a department store.

Many people find their way to wedding consulting after careers as events coordinators and planners, or after working weddings as caterers, florists, and musicians. If you have already developed relationships with area vendors and others involved in the planning of weddings, you may be able to start your own business without the aid of a professional organization. But if you're new to the business, it's best to go through a training program for certification. Not only will you receive instruction and professional advice, but you'll receive referrals from the organization.

With guidance, training, and a clear understanding of the responsibilities of the job, a wedding consultant can command a good fee from the onset of a new business. Start-up costs are relatively low, since you can easily work from your home with a computer, an extra phone line, and some advertising. You might want to invest in some basic software to maintain a database, to make attractive graphics for presentation purposes, and to access the Internet. Formal and semiformal dress wear is also important, as you'll be attending many different kinds of weddings.

ADVANCEMENT

As you gain experience as a consultant, you'll be able to expand your business and clientele. You'll develop relationships with area vendors that will result in more referrals and better discounts. With a bigger business, you can hire regular staff members to help you with planning, running errands, and administrative duties. Some consultants expand their services to include such perks as calligraphic invitations and specially designed favors for receptions. Many consultants, including Packy Boukis (http://www.clevelandwedding.com), maintain Web sites to promote their businesses and provide wedding advice. Packy Boukis has already expanded her expertise to the Web and other media, providing interviews for *Modern Bride* and the *Wall Street Journal*. She would like to someday put together a packet of informative books for brides.

EARNINGS

Due to the fairly recent development of wedding consulting as a career, there are no comprehensive salary surveys available. Also, the number of uncertified consultants, and consultants who only plan weddings part time, makes it difficult to estimate average earnings. According to the Association of Certified Professional Wedding Consultants, consultants earn between $25,000 to $60,000 or more.

Though consultants make between 10 to 20 percent of a wedding's expense, consultants generally charge a flat rate. Robbi Ernst, founder of June Wedding Inc., has maintained a survey of consulting fees over the last 14 years. He places initial consultation fees at $275 to $425 per session, with a session lasting about three hours. A consultant may also be hired to oversee all the prewedding administrative details for between $1,000 and $2,000. A consultant who works the wedding day only will charge between $1,200 and $1,800. For a complete package, with assistance in the months before the wedding and up through the reception, a consultant will charge $3,000 or more. "These fees are based on educated and trained wedding consultants," Ernst says. "Our survey finds that people who have formally trained and certified can get these fees from the onset of their business if they are professional and know what they're doing."

These fees are based on consultants in metropolitan areas with populations of 500,000 or more. In a large city, an experienced consultant can realistically expect to have a wedding planned for every weekend. Because destination weddings are usually much smaller than traditional weddings, consulting fees are lower.

Wedding and party consultants who work for a company usually receive benefits such as health and life insurance, vacation days, sick leave, and a savings and pension program. Self-employed consultants must provide their own benefits.

WORK ENVIRONMENT

For someone who loves weddings and meeting new people, consulting can be an ideal career. Your clients may be stressed out occasionally, but most of the time they're going to be enthusiastic about planning their weddings. During the week, your hours will be spent meeting with vendors, taking phone calls, and working at the computer. Your weekends will be a bit faster paced, among larger crowds, and you'll get to see the results of your hard work—you'll be at the wedding sites, fussing over final details and making sure everything goes smoothly.

Your office hours won't be affected by weather conditions, but on the actual wedding days you'll be expected to get easily and quickly from one place to the other. Bad weather on the day of an outdoor wedding can result in more work for you as you move everything to the "rain site." One of the perks of wedding consulting is taking an active part in someone's celebration; part of your job is making sure everyone has a good time. But you'll also be expected to be present for weddings, receptions, and rehearsal dinners, which means you'll be working weekends and occasional evenings.

OUTLOOK

More than 2.4 million weddings are held each year in the United States alone, according to the Association of Bridal Consultants, which suggests that there are good employment opportunities for certified wedding planners. According to Robbi Ernst of June Wedding Inc., the people getting married for the first time are older, better educated, and more sophisticated. They're paying for their own weddings and have more original ideas for their ceremonies. Also, more people are celebrating their anniversaries by renewing their vows with large events. Wedding consultants will want to capitalize on this trend, as well as expand into other ceremonies like bar and bat mitzvahs.

The growth of the Internet and related technology will continue to change the world of wedding consulting. Some consultants may design their own wedding invitations and related materials with the assistance of desktop publishing software. Many wedding consultants have established Web sites that detail their services and help couples plan their weddings. Consultants who are proficient with computer technology, including design software, will have the best employment opportunities.

FOR MORE INFORMATION

For information on home study and professional designations, contact
Association of Bridal Consultants
56 Danbury Road, Suite 11
New Milford, CT 06776
Tel: 860-355-7000
Email: office@bridalassn.com
http://www.bridalassn.com

For information on training programs and certification, contact
Association of Certified Professional Wedding Consultants
7791 Prestwick Circle
San Jose, CA 95135-2142
Tel: 408-528-9000
Email: anola@acpwc.com
http://www.acpwc.com

Visit the June Wedding Web site for training and certification information.
June Wedding Inc.
19375 Pine Glade
Guerneville, CA 95446-9046
Tel: 707-865-9894
http://www.junewedding.com

For information on training programs, home study, and certification, contact
National Bridal Service
1004 North Thompson Street, Suite 205
Richmond, VA 23230-4926
Tel: 804-342-0055
http://www.nationalbridal.com

Index

Entries and page numbers in **bold** indicate major treatment of a topic.